Who bears the tax burden in the United States? How has the distribution of taxes changed in the past two decades? What changes have occurred in the distribution of income before and after taxes?

This book reports the results of a long-term program of research on the distribution of tax burdens. The analysis is based on a unique series of microdata sets developed by merging the information from the annual consumer population surveys of the U.S. Census Bureau and the tax returns filed with the Internal Revenue Service.

The first results of this research program were presented in *Who Bears the Tax Burden?* (Brookings, 1974), which presented estimates of the distribution of federal, state, and local taxes in 1966. In this sequel to the 1974 volume, Joseph A. Pechman presents estimates for 1970, 1975, 1980, and 1985. The study concludes that the tax system became less progressive between 1966 and 1985, primarily because the corporation income and property taxes declined in importance while heavier emphasis was being placed on the payroll tax.

The author, a noted tax expert, was formerly director of Economic Studies and is now a senior fellow in the Economic Studies program at Brookings. He has written extensively on fiscal and tax matters and has been in the forefront of the movement to broaden the income tax base and lower the marginal tax rates.

Studies of Government Finance: Second Series

TITLES PUBLISHED

Who Paid the Taxes, 1966–85?

JOSEPH A. PECHMAN

Studies of Government Finance

THE BROOKINGS INSTITUTION

WASHINGTON, D.C.

Copyright © 1985 by
THE BROOKINGS INSTITUTION
1775 Massachusetts Avenue, N.W. Washington, D.C. 20036

Library of Congress Cataloging in Publication data:

Pechman, Joseph A., 1918–
  Who paid the taxes. 1966–85?
  (Studies of government finance. Second series)
  Includes bibliographical references and index.
  1. Tax incidence—United States.   2. Taxation—
United States.   I. Title.   II. Series.
HJ2322.A3P42   1985   336.2'94'0973   83-45845
ISBN 0-8157-6998-9
ISBN 0-8157-6997-0 (pbk.)
9 8 7 6 5 4 3 2 1

THE BROOKINGS INSTITUTION is an independent organization devoted to nonpartisan research, education, and publication in economics, government, foreign policy, and the social sciences generally. Its principal purposes are to aid in the development of sound public policies and to promote public understanding of issues of national importance.

The Institution was founded on December 8, 1927, to merge the activities of the Institute for Government Research, founded in 1916, the Institute of Economics, founded in 1922, and the Robert Brookings Graduate School of Economics and Government, founded in 1924.

The Board of Trustees is responsible for the general administration of the Institution, while the immediate direction of the policies, program, and staff is vested in the President, assisted by an advisory committee of the officers and staff. The by-laws of the Institution state: "It is the function of the Trustees to make possible the conduct of scientific research, and publication, under the most favorable conditions, and to safeguard the independence of the research staff in the pursuit of their studies and in the publication of the results of such studies. It is not a part of their function to determine, control, or influence the conduct of particular investigations or the conclusions reached."

The President bears final responsibility for the decision to publish a manuscript as a Brookings book. In reaching his judgment on the competence, accuracy, and objectivity of each study, the President is advised by the director of the appropriate research program and weighs the views of a panel of expert outside readers who report to him in confidence on the quality of the work. Publication of a work signifies that it is deemed a competent treatment worthy of public consideration but does not imply endorsement of conclusions or recommendations.

The Institution maintains its position of neutrality on issues of public policy in order to safeguard the intellectual freedom of the staff. Hence interpretations or conclusions in Brookings publications should be understood to be solely those of the authors and should not be attributed to the Institution, to its trustees, officers, or other staff members, or to the organizations that support its research.

11/7/69

To my mother and father

Foreword

THE DISTRIBUTION of tax burdens by income class is of major concern to the general public, political leaders, and social scientists, yet the information regarding this distribution is scanty. The lack of information is attributable to the difficulty of making such estimates and to the conceptual problems of deciding who actually pays the various taxes. Although the analytical framework used by tax economists has greatly improved in recent years, there are still significant differences of opinion about who bears the burden of the major components of modern tax systems.

To assist in understanding who pays the taxes, the Brookings Institution has sponsored a long-term statistical research program on the distribution of tax burdens based on a series of microdata sets especially designed for this type of analysis. These data sets were developed by merging the information from the annual current population surveys of the U.S. Bureau of the Census and the tax return samples of the Internal Revenue Service. When properly weighted, the incomes and taxes allocated to the sample units in these MERGE files aggregate to the national totals. The data base permits calculations of tax burdens on the basis of eight sets of incidence assumptions that span the range of opinion held by most economists.

The first results of this research program were published in 1974 in a Brookings book by Joseph A. Pechman and Benjamin A. Okner (*Who Bears the Tax Burden?*), which presented estimates of the distribution of federal, state, and local tax burdens in 1966. Since then, MERGE files have been developed for 1970 and 1975, and projections have been made from the 1975 file to 1980 and 1985. Thus it is now possible to trace the changes in the distribution of tax burdens over a period of almost two decades, from 1966 to 1985.

In a real sense this volume by Joseph A. Pechman is a sequel to *Who Bears the Tax Burden?* For many of the technical details on how the MERGE files are prepared, the interested reader is referred to the appendixes in the 1974 volume. Chapters 2 and 3 have been reproduced from the 1974 volume with only slight modifications.

Many talented and imaginative people contributed to this project. Two key members were equal partners with the author in planning and executing the enterprise: Benjamin A. Okner, who supervised the preparation of the 1966 and 1970 files, and Joseph J. Minarik, who oversaw the development of the 1975 file. John Karl Scholz completed the 1975 file and prepared the projections for 1980 and 1985. The programming group consisted of Catherine Armington, Christine C. de Fontenay, Marjorie P. Odle, Nancy E. O'Hara, Jon K. Peck, and George Sadowsky, and the principal research assistants were Timothy A. Cohn, Barry J. Eichengreen, Peter Gould, Mark J. Mazur, Andrew D. Pike, Ralph W. Tryon, and John Yinger.

The author is grateful to the original reading committee, George F. Break, Robert J. Lampman, and Richard A. Musgrave. Arnold C. Harberger, Charles E. McLure, Jr., and Peter Mieszkowski, who played key roles in the development of modern tax theory, read the original manuscript and made numerous useful suggestions. Thoughtful comments on this volume were received from Barry P. Bosworth, Gary Burtless, Richard Goode, Charles E. McLure, Jr., and John Karl Scholz. Harold S. Appelman verified the factual content and greatly improved the accuracy. The manuscript was edited by Karen J. Wirt and was keyboarded for computer typesetting by Susan F. Woollen and Vickie L. Corey. Nancy Snyder proofread the book, and Ward & Silvan prepared the index.

The basic work on the files was begun under the Brookings program of Studies of Government Finance, which was supported by a grant from the Ford Foundation. The work on the distribution of tax burdens was financed by grants from the U.S. Office of Economic Opportunity and the National Science Foundation. The manuscript for this volume was prepared while the author was a visiting scholar at the Hoover Institution, Stanford University, in the academic year 1983–84, and during the summer of 1984 when he was visiting Dwight Ankeny professor of economics at Dartmouth College. The work on the book was supported by grants from the Ford Foundation and the Alfred P. Sloan Foundation.

BRUCE K. MACLAURY
President

December 1984
Washington, D.C.

Contents

Appendix Tables

Figures

CHAPTER ONE

Introduction and Summary

THE TAXES paid by the nation's family units to the federal, state, and local governments amounted to more than $700 billion in 1980, or over 25 percent of total family income.[1] Strong views are held as to whether the burden of these taxes is distributed fairly by income class or among persons with substantially equal incomes. Some believe that the tax system is regressive; others consider it to be progressive.[2] Still others are concerned not only about the equity of the tax system across income classes (vertical equity), but also about its equity among those with the same income (horizontal equity). To a large extent, the debate has centered around the individual income tax, which is the largest source of government revenue in the United States. Even though the other taxes account for more than twice the revenue produced by the individual income tax, the distribution of these taxes by income classes is not generally known. Nor is it generally known if the tax system as a whole has become more or less progressive in recent years. The purpose of this study is to estimate the effect of all U.S. taxes on the distribution of income and how this distribution has changed in the last two decades.

Major Features of the Study

Although others have made similar estimates,[3] this study is unique in three respects. First, the estimates are based on microunit data files for representa-

1. This ratio is lower than the commonly cited ratio of government receipts to the national income primarily because taxes exclude receipts from nontax sources. See chapter 2 for a detailed explanation of the term "taxes" as used in this study.
2. A tax is *regressive* when the ratio of tax to income falls as incomes rise; a tax is *proportional* when the ratio of tax to income is the same for all income classes; and a tax is *progressive* when the ratio of tax to income rises as incomes rise.
3. For a list of the most important studies of tax incidence, see chapter 3, note 1.

tive samples of families (referred to as the MERGE files);[4] when properly weighted, the samples account for the estimated total income received by family units in the United States. In addition to data on income, the files contain demographic and other economic information about each of the sample units (for example, home ownership, place of residence, age of family members, and so on). This information is available on computer tape and can be processed quickly and efficiently on an electronic computer, thus permitting estimates to be prepared in more detail than was possible with the previous data-processing techniques.

Second, although progress has been made in recent years in improving the methodology of tax analysis, economists still disagree about the incidence of several of the most important taxes in the tax system. Instead of limiting the analysis to one or a few views, estimates were prepared on the basis of eight sets of assumptions that span the range of opinions currently held by most economists.

Third, MERGE files have been developed for the years 1966, 1970, and 1975, and the 1975 file has been projected to 1980 and 1985. Thus the data provide estimates of the changes in the distribution of tax burdens over a period of about two decades.

The income concept used here corresponds closely to an economist's comprehensive definition of income for family units. In addition to the incomes earned in the market system (wages, interest, dividends, rents, and business profits), this concept includes transfer payments and capital gains accrued during the year (whether realized or not).[5] To convert income to a before-tax basis, indirect business taxes, as well as direct taxes, are included in income.[6]

The "incidence" of a tax—a term that is used synonymously with "tax burden" in this study—is measured by the reduction in real incomes that results from the imposition of that tax. Taxes affect real income in either or both of two ways. They may reduce the incomes of individuals in their role as producers; or they may increase the prices of consumer goods and thus reduce the purchasing power of a given amount of money income. The former effect is the burden of taxation on the "sources" of income; the latter is the burden

4. In this book the term "families" refers both to individuals living alone (one-person families) and to the conventional family consisting of two or more persons, related by blood, marriage, or adoption.

5. Gifts and bequests should also be included in income, but these were omitted because little is known about their distribution among families.

6. Direct taxes are automatically included in factor incomes; indirect taxes were allocated to individual family units in proportion to their shares of factor incomes. For the rationale of this procedure, see chapter 3.

on the "uses" of income. Both of these effects are measured in this study. However, no attempt is made to measure the burden that results from the reallocation of resources or the changes in consumption patterns that may be caused by taxation because such effects cannot be measured with sufficient accuracy.

This book is concerned solely with the distribution of tax burdens, without any reference to the distribution of benefits from the governmental activities that are supported by taxes. It attempts to show how the distribution of disposable income in the past two decades differed from what the distribution would have been if all tax revenues had come from a proportional income tax with the same yields.[7] This differential incidence approach was adopted because the benefits of many, if not most, government activities cannot be allocated even in principle.[8] However, transfers by government to individuals (social security and unemployment benefits, welfare payments, workmen's compensation, food stamps, medicare, and medicaid) can be allocated to family units, and this allocation is made here.

The remainder of this chapter summarizes the major findings of the study. Chapter 2 describes the basic concepts and methods, and chapter 3 discusses the rationale of the different sets of assumptions used to distribute the various taxes to individual family units. Chapter 4 summarizes the distribution of tax burdens by income class in 1980; chapter 5 discusses the changes in this distribution that occurred from 1966 to 1985.

Distribution of Tax Burdens, 1980

The major conclusions of this study may be seen in figure 1-1, which shows the 1980 effective rates of tax by population percentiles ranked according to income for the most progressive and the least progressive sets of

7. The differences between actual effective rates and the effective rate of a proportional income tax are not actually shown in any of the tables or figures in this study; they can easily be derived by subtraction.

8. Many governmental activities produce "public goods" (for example, national defense), the benefits of which to any specific individual cannot be evaluated. For a discussion of the problems of measuring the benefits of government expenditures, see J. Margolis and H. Guitton, eds., *Public Economics: An Analysis of Public Production and Consumption and Their Relations to the Private Sectors* (Macmillan, 1969). For the logically correct method of distributing the benefits of public goods, see Henry Aaron and Martin McGuire, "Public Goods and Income Distribution," *Econometrica*, vol. 38 (November 1970). This method cannot be applied because information on consumer preferences for public goods is not available.

Figure 1-1. *Effective Rates of Federal, State, and Local Taxes under the Most and Least Progressive Incidence Variants, by Population Percentile, 1980*

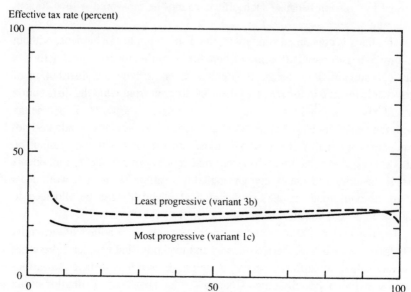

Effective tax rate (percent)

Least progressive (variant 3b)

Most progressive (variant 1c)

Population percentile[a]

Source: Brookings MERGE file. For an explanation of the incidence variants see table 3-1.
a. Arrayed by size of adjusted family income.

incidence assumptions used.[9] Under the most progressive assumptions (variant 1c) effective tax rates in 1980 ran from about 20 percent at the lowest end of the income scale to 27 percent at the top. Under the least progressive assumptions (variant 3b) effective tax rates declined from over 30 percent at the lowest end of the distribution to about 25 percent in the second decile and remained at that level until they declined to 22 percent in the top percentile. For the distribution as a whole, the tax system was either moderately progressive (variant 1c) or slightly regressive (variant 3b). The differences in effective rates between the two variants were relatively small except at the bottom of the income scale, where the tax burden was much higher under variant 3b than it was under 1c, and at the top, where the tax burden was higher under variant 1c.

Because the degree of progressivity or regressivity is relatively small under any of the incidence assumptions, it is clear that the tax system has very little

9. The 1980 effective rates are used here because this was the latest year for which actual tax collections were available to prepare the MERGE file. The 1985 file, to be discussed below, is based on budget projections of tax receipts. See chapter 2 for an explanation of the methods used to prepare the 1980 and 1985 files.

Figure 1-2. *Lorenz Curves of the Distributions of Adjusted Family Income before and after Federal, State, and Local Taxes and Transfers under the Most Progressive Variant 1c, 1980*

Cumulative percent of income

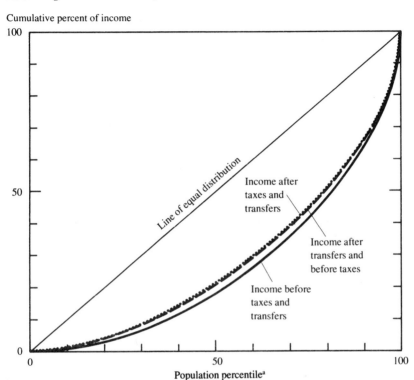

Population percentile[a]

Source: Brookings MERGE file. Taxes are based on variant 1c assumptions. For an explanation of the incidence variants see table 3-1.

a. Arrayed by size of market income.

effect on the distribution of income. However, the system of transfer payments is highly progressive and has a major effect on the income distribution. This is illustrated in figure 1-2, which shows the Lorenz curves for the 1980 distributions of income before and after transfers and taxes when taxes are allocated under variant 1c assumptions.[10] As might be expected in the case of a progressive tax and transfer system, the Lorenz curve for the distribution of after-tax and after-transfer income under variant 1c lies 10 percent closer to the line of equal distribution than the before-tax curve. But the movement

10. A Lorenz curve shows the cumulative percentage of the aggregate income received by any given cumulative percentage of recipients arrayed by the size of their incomes. When all income recipients receive the same income, the Lorenz curve is a straight line with a slope of 45 degrees. As the distribution becomes more unequal, the Lorenz curve moves downward and to the right, away from the line of equal distribution.

toward equality for the tax system alone was small—2.5 percent under variant 1c and considerably smaller percentages under the other variants examined in this study. In the case of variant 3b—the least progressive set of assumptions—the after-tax distribution differed only slightly from the before-tax distribution (it was 0.9 percent less equal). The change was so small that the Lorenz curves for the two distributions cannot be distinguished on the scale used in figure 1-2.

The incidence assumptions of variant 1c were more progressive than those of 3b largely because of differences in the treatment of the corporation income tax and the property tax. Under 1c, these two taxes are assumed to be taxes on income from capital,[11] while under 3b half of the corporation income tax and half of the property tax on improvements are assumed to be paid by consumers through increases in the relative prices of housing and other goods and services.[12] Since property income is heavily concentrated among families in the highest income classes, effective tax rates under the variant 1c assumptions rise as incomes rise. On the other hand, the average effective rate of tax under variant 3b is virtually proportional for the lower 90 percent of the income distribution and regressive only in the top 10 percent because the ratio of consumption to income falls as incomes rise. Relative tax burdens under all other variants examined in this study also depend heavily on the assumptions made with respect to the incidence of the corporation income tax and the property tax.

The crucial nature of the incidence assumptions for the corporation income tax and the property tax is also revealed when effective rates are shown separately for federal taxes and state-local taxes (see figure 1-3). Because the federal government relies greatly on the individual income tax and the corporation income tax, average effective federal tax rates are progressive except at the top of the income scale, where they decline slightly. This pattern holds whether the corporation income tax is borne by owners of capital or is partly shifted to consumers. On the other hand, state-local tax rates are regressive at the low end of the income distribution, roughly proportional between the second and the ninth decile, and progressive in the top decile if the corpora-

11. The assumption under variant 1c is that half of the corporation income tax is borne by corporate stockholders and the other half is borne by owners of capital in general.

12. Under both variants the individual income tax is assumed to be borne by the income recipients; sales taxes and excises are assumed to be paid by consumers; and employee payroll taxes are assumed to be paid by the workers. Other differences between the two variants are that the property tax on land is assumed to be paid by owners of capital in general under variant 1c and by landowners under 3b, and that the employer payroll tax is borne by employees under 1c and shifted to the consumer under 3b. However, these differences have a relatively small effect on the distribution of tax burdens.

Figure 1-3. *Effective Rates of Federal and of State and Local Taxes under the Most and Least Progressive Variants, by Population Percentile, 1980*

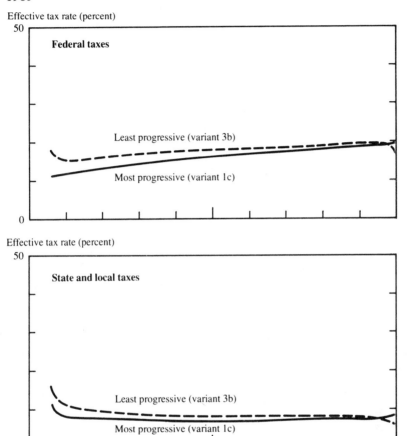

Source: Brookings MERGE file. For an explanation of the incidence variants see table 3-1.
a. Arrayed by size of adjusted family income.

tion income tax and the property tax are regarded as taxes on capital, or regressive if they are partly a tax on consumption.[13]

13. In addition to differences that arise because of differences in incidence assumptions, there are substantial variations in tax rates among various economic and demographic groups in the population that are due to the structural features of the U.S. tax system. For example, home owners pay lower taxes than do renters, urban residents pay somewhat higher taxes than residents of rural-farm areas, and married couples pay lower taxes than single persons. See Joseph A. Pechman and Benjamin A. Okner, *Who Bears the Tax Burden?* (Brookings, 1974), chap. 5.

The relative tax burdens imposed on income from labor and from capital also depend on the incidence assumptions for the corporation income tax and the property tax. If these taxes are assumed to be taxes on capital, income from capital bears a slightly heavier tax than income from labor. For example, under variant 1c, the effective tax rate on income from capital was 21.5 percent in 1980 compared to 19.9 percent for income from labor. But the relative burdens are reversed if the corporation income tax and the property tax are assumed to be paid in whole or in part by consumers. Thus, under variant 3b, income from capital paid an average tax rate of 14.6 percent, while labor income paid a tax of 18.1 percent. Labor and capital both bear a lower tax burden under variant 3b than under 1c because the burden on consumption is higher—20.5 percent compared with 9.7 percent in 1980.[14]

Changes in the Distribution of Tax Burdens, 1966–85

The major influences on the distribution of tax burdens between 1966 and 1985 were a decline in the relative importance of the corporation income tax and the property tax and a rise in payroll taxes. Since the former two are progressive tax sources and the latter is regressive, the effect of these changes was to reduce the progressivity of the tax system. The federal tax cuts in 1981 also contributed to the reduction in progressivity. Between 1966 and 1985 tax burdens increased in the lower part of the income scale, declined sharply at the top, and remained roughly the same or rose slightly in between. The effective tax rate in the highest population decile fell from 1.79 times the burden in the lowest decile in 1966 to 1.16 in 1985 under variant 1c and from 0.94 to 0.83 under variant 3b (figure 1-4).

The decline in the progressivity of the tax system during this period was caused by a decline in the progressivity of federal taxes. State and local taxes became somewhat more progressive or retained the same degree of progressivity, depending on the incidence assumptions. Individual income taxes remained progressive throughout the period, but less so at the end of the period than at the beginning because of the effect of "bracket creep" resulting from the growth of real incomes as well as inflation and the federal tax cuts enacted in 1981.

In 1966 the tax burden on capital income was substantially higher than the burden on labor income. This pattern was reversed by 1985 as a result of the

14. In these calculations total taxes were allocated to three categories: labor income, capital income, and consumption.

Figure 1-4. *Effective Rates of Federal, State, and Local Taxes under the Most and Least Progressive Incidence Variants, by Population Percentile, 1966 and 1985*

Effective tax rate (percent)

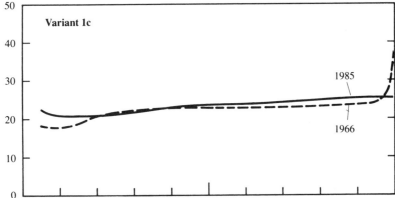

Effective tax rate (percent)

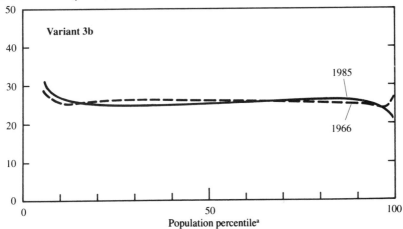

Population percentile[a]

Source: Brookings MERGE files. For an explanation of the incidence variants see table 3-1.
a. Arrayed by size of family income.

reduced roles of the corporation income tax and the property tax and the greater role of the payroll tax.

There was virtually no change in the distribution of income as defined in this study between 1966 and 1985. However, this income concept includes transfer payments, which rose dramatically during this period. As a result, the distribution of income from market activity (wages and salaries, interest, dividends, rents, and windfall profits) must have become more unequal.

Because the tax system became less progressive, the distribution of income *after* taxes and transfers was more unequal in 1985 than in 1966.

Summary

The U.S. tax system is either moderately progressive or slightly regressive, depending on the incidence assumptions for the major taxes. If the corporation income tax and the property tax are assumed to be borne by capital, the very rich pay higher average effective tax rates than does the average family. If these taxes are assumed to be shifted to consumers to a considerable degree, the very rich pay lower effective rates than the average family.

The tax system has relatively little effect on the distribution of income. In contrast, the transfer system has a significant equalizing effect.

The tax system became less progressive between 1966 and 1985, primarily because the corporation income tax and the property tax declined in importance while more emphasis was placed on the payroll tax.

CHAPTER TWO

Concepts and Methodology

THE FINDINGS presented in chapter 1 depend on definitions and assumptions that are discussed there only briefly. Because an accurate appraisal of the results and their implications requires a thorough understanding of what is being measured and compared, this chapter explains in some detail the concepts and methodology used in this study. The unique sets of data for individual family units that were especially created for the study are also described.

Definition of Terms

To the average citizen, the terms "income" and "taxes" may seem self-explanatory. Income is the sum of the earnings received for services rendered and the return on the investment of capital; taxes are the amounts individuals are obliged to pay to the government. These are also the definitions that the economist would apply in the case of most individuals; however, they ignore many complications that arise from the intricacies of a modern economy and the government's relationship to the taxpayer.

Income

Economists define income as the amount an individual can spend during a particular time period and still have the same net assets (valued in money terms) at the end of the period as at the beginning. Another way of saying the same thing is that income is the amount of an individual's consumption outlays plus the increase (or minus the decrease) in that person's net worth during a particular time period.[1] Although this definition is almost universally accepted by economists, no government or private agency provides regular

1. See Henry C. Simons, *Personal Income Taxation: The Definition of Income as a Problem of Fiscal Policy* (University of Chicago Press, 1938), chap. 2. Outlays include tax payments on income as well as the taxes that are paid as part of the market price of consumption goods and

11

estimates of income on the basis of this concept.[2] The closest approach is the national income series published by the U.S. Department of Commerce.[3] Family income—the income measure from which the analysis in this study begins—was derived from the national income series.[4]

National income is the value, at factor costs, of the goods and services produced by the nation's economy. It includes employees' compensation, proprietors' income, net interest, net rental income of individuals, and corporate profits before taxes. Transfer payments, gifts and bequests, and increases in the value of capital assets would have to be added to make this concept correspond to the economists' definition of income for a household unit.[5] As defined in this study, family income includes transfer payments and capital gains accrued during the year (whether realized or not) but does not include gifts and bequests because of the difficulty of estimating them reliably. In addition, since the analysis is confined to family units, two kinds of income are excluded from family income—income received by persons in the institutional population and by pension funds and nonprofit organizations and income retained by fiduciaries.[6]

The national income accounts provide estimates of transfer payments but not of capital gains.[7] Such gains were estimated separately for corporate stock

services. In principle, an individual's net worth includes the value of human as well as physical capital; but changes in the value of human capital are excluded from this study because there are no data on the amount and distribution of human capital and because changes in the value of human capital are not generally regarded as an appropriate part of an income tax base.

2. The author of this study and two colleagues made such estimates for the year 1972 and 1985, with some modifications. See Joseph A. Pechman and Benjamin A. Okner, "Individual Income Tax Erosion by Income Classes," in *The Economics of Federal Subsidy Programs*, A Compendium of Papers submitted to the Joint Economic Committee, pt. 1, *General Study Papers*, 92 Cong. 2 sess. (1972), pp. 13–40 (Brookings Reprint 230); and Joseph A. Pechman and John Karl Scholz, "Comprehensive Income Taxation and Rate Reduction," *Tax Notes*, October 11, 1982 (Brookings Reprint 390).

3. U.S. Department of Commerce, Office of Business Economics, *National Income, 1954 Edition* (U.S. Government Printing Office, 1954), p. 58.

4. As is noted below in this chapter and in chapter 3, the appropriate concept for measuring tax burdens—which will be called "adjusted family income"—depends upon the incidence assumptions for the various taxes.

5. Gifts are regarded as any other consumption outlay by the donor and are, therefore, not deductible in computing the donor's income. See Simons, *Personal Income Taxation*, pp. 57–58.

6. The only other departure from the official definition of national income is the omission of interest imputed to individuals for the services rendered to them by the banking system. For a more detailed description of the concept of family income, see Joseph A. Pechman and Benjamin A. Okner, *Who Bears the Tax Burden?* (Brookings, 1974), app. A.

7. Interest payments by the federal government are regarded as transfer payments in the national income accounts. Consequently, these are included in the transfer payments that are added to national income in deriving family income.

and for other assets. In the case of corporate stock, it was assumed that the retained earnings of corporations—which are given in the national income accounts—are a rough approximation of the gains that accrued on their stock during the year. In other words, corporate retained earnings were substituted for realized capital gains reported on the tax returns of the family units in the sample. This approximation was used instead of the change in the value of corporate stock during the year because stock values fluctuate widely and even averages of three to five years may not give an adequate representation of accrued capital gains. However, over long periods of time, capital gains on corporate securities are roughly equal to retained earnings.[8] In the case of other assets it was necessary to combine estimates of changes in the value of business inventories, farm assets, and nonfarm real estate. Changes in the value of business inventories are given in the national income accounts; changes in the value of farm assets and nonfarm real estate were estimated on the basis of other sources.[9]

The decision to approximate capital gains on corporate stock by the amount of retained corporate earnings means that family income includes all corporation profits before tax. In addition to retained earnings, these profits include dividends and corporate profits tax liabilities. Dividends are included in family income because they are direct receipts of household units; the corporation income tax is included on the assumption that it is borne by stockholders;[10] and retained earnings are included as a measure of capital gains.[11] This procedure has the advantage of providing not only consistency with the concept of national income, but also a complete accounting of the accrued income claims of the household sector.

Family income excludes some receipts that are usually regarded as income and includes some that are received in nonmoney form. Excluded are receipts from private pensions and annuities and government retirement benefits (such as civil service pensions) that are not financed through payroll taxes. Private and public employer contributions to funds for such benefits are considered

8. See Martin J. Bailey, "Capital Gains and Income Taxation," in Arnold C. Harberger and Martin J. Bailey, eds., *The Taxation of Income from Capital* (Brookings, 1969); and Martin David, *Alternative Approaches to Capital Gains Taxation* (Brookings, 1968), pp. 242–46.

9. For the method of estimation see Pechman and Okner, *Who Bears the Tax Burden?* app. A.

10. Under certain assumptions the corporation tax is considered to be a tax on capital generally, on consumption, or on corporate wages and salaries. See chapter 3.

11. Corporate profits before tax are *not* adjusted for the change in the value of inventories. Such gains (or losses) on inventories correspond to capital gains and losses on other assets, which are included in family income.

part of family income during the year in which the contributions are made;[12] later, when payments are received, they are viewed as representing only a change in the form of asset holding by families (that is, cash is increased, and a prepaid insurance asset is reduced). On the other hand, payments to families financed through payroll taxes or general government revenue (for example, social security benefits and welfare payments) are considered transfers and are included in family income. Similarly, supplements to wages and salaries to finance health and other welfare benefits are counted as income in the year they are set aside by the employer and not in the year when the benefits are received.[13] The major forms of nonmoney income that are included in income are unrealized capital gains, net imputed rent on owner-occupied dwellings, the value of food stamps, medicare, and medicaid.

The derivation of family income from national income is shown in table 2-1. In 1980, national income amounted to $2,121 billion. To convert this figure to an estimate of family income it is necessary to add transfer payments of $252 billion and accrued capital gains on business inventories, farm assets, and nonfarm real estate of $352 billion.[14] Income not received by families in the household sector, which amounted to $95 billion, is then subtracted, leaving family income of $2,630 billion.

Taxes

The definition of taxes in this study is similar to that of government receipts as defined in the national income accounts. However, since government receipts is a more comprehensive concept than taxes, nontax revenues were excluded from the tax measure. In addition, tax payments attributed to institutions or organizations not in the household sector were excluded, and customs duties and estate and gift taxes were omitted from the tax concept.

12. The federal government does not make current contributions to a fund for military retirement pay, but pays benefits out of general revenues when military personnel retire. An allowance for the accrued rights of such personnel was not made because no data were available for making an estimate.

13. The model for this pattern of exclusion and inclusion is that of a private insurance system in which the equities of each individual are preserved. In fact, few private plans or plans for government employees are so designed, and benefits ultimately received by any particular employee bear little relation to the contributions made on that person's behalf. Moreover, benefits exceed the amounts originally set aside by the employers because of interest earnings on the contributions.

14. Since income is defined in current dollars, the national income adjustments for inventory valuation and capital consumption are reversed. This adjustment is included with accrued capital gains in table 2-1.

Table 2-1. *Derivation of Family Income from National Income, 1980*
Billions of dollars

Description	Amount
National income (as defined in the national income accounts)	**2,121**
Additions to national income	
Transfer payments to persons[a]	252
Accrued capital gains on business inventories, farm assets, and nonfarm real estate[b]	352
Deductions from national income	
Income not received by families[c]	95
Family Income	**2,630**

Source: Author's estimates based on data in *Survey of Current Business*, June 1982, pp. 6, 9.

a. Includes net interest payments by the federal government and by consumers, which are regarded as transfer payments in the national income accounts.

b. Includes the inventory valuation and capital consumption adjustments.

c. Includes income of persons in the military and institutional population and property income received by fiduciaries, pension funds, and nonprofit organizations.

With minor exceptions, the procedure used here was to accept the national income accounts definitions for classifying tax and nontax receipts.[15] In 1980, total federal, state, and local government receipts amounted to $837 billion, while taxes as defined here were $716 billion. (See table 2-2.)

Nontax receipts include personal and business nontax receipts, some items that are regarded as social insurance receipts in the national income accounts, and an assortment of state-local fees and licenses. Nontax receipts from individuals are primarily charges for tuition at state colleges and universities and local hospital fees, while nontax receipts from businesses include rents and royalties and an assortment of fees collected for various government services.[16] The excluded social insurance receipts are payments to civilian government retirement plans, which resemble private pension plans. They are omitted because payments into such plans are not taxes; they are regarded as payments on behalf of individuals for the purchase of future retirement benefits. Miscellaneous receipts of state and local governments consist primarily of marriage license fees, charges for dog licenses, and similar items.

About one-fourth of all corporate stock is owned by fiduciaries and other

15. The net receipts of government enterprises, such as profits from state liquor stores and public utilities, were also excluded from the tax concept used in this study, since these receipts are largely payments for goods received.

16. An exception was made in the case of government receipts from persons for motor vehicle licenses. These were included in the tax concept (as is done in the national income accounts) even though this levy might be defined as a user charge.

Table 2-2. *Derivation of Federal, State, and Local Taxes*
from Total National Income Receipts, 1980
Billions of dollars

Description	Amount
Federal, state, and local government receipts[a]	**837**
Deductions for this study	
Personal and business nontax receipts	41
Corporate profits taxes of organizations not in household population	21
Nontax social insurance contribution receipts	41
Miscellaneous state and local receipts	1
Federal customs duties	7
Estate, gift, and death taxes	9
Total deductions	121
Federal, state, and local taxes **(as defined in this study)**	**716**

Source: Author's estimates based on data in *Survey of Current Business*, June 1982, pp. 6, 9. Figures are rounded.
a. As defined in the national income accounts; adjusted to exclude the duplication of federal grants-in-aid to state and local governments.

organizations that are not represented in the family population. Total corporation tax accruals were reduced by $21 billion to reflect the amounts that are not borne by family units in the household sector.

The last two adjustments—the exclusion of customs duties and of estate and gift taxes—were made for special reasons. In the case of customs duties, the exclusion was based on the presumption that these duties are levied primarily to discourage imports rather than to increase government income.[17] In the case of the estate and gift taxes, it makes little sense to distribute death taxes among people who have died, since they no longer exist in the population. Logic would suggest that death and gift taxes be allocated among the new owners of the property that was transferred. However, this would require that the amount of the gift or bequest upon which the tax was levied also be distributed among such persons. There is little statistical information available on families who receive gifts or bequests and therefore no reliable basis upon which to allocate either the assets transferred or the taxes collected.[18]

17. The decision to exclude customs receipts from taxes is a close one. Since they amount to only about 1 percent of total tax receipts, the conclusions of this study would not be altered if they were included.

18. Rough estimates of the effect of including estate and gift taxes are given in Pechman and Okner, *Who Bears the Tax Burden?* app. C.

Table 2-3. *Federal, State, and Local Taxes, by Source, 1980*
Billions of dollars

Source	Federal taxes	State and local taxes	Total
Personal taxes	249	50	299
Income taxes	249	45	294
Other[a]	. . .	4	4
Corporate profits taxes	52	9	61
Indirect business taxes	29	165	194
State and local general sales taxes	. . .	67	67
Gasoline excise taxes	5	10	15
Liquor excise taxes	6	3	8
Tobacco excise taxes	3	4	6
Other excise taxes	6	. . .	6
Windfall profits tax	10	. . .	10
Motor vehicle licenses	. . .	2	2
Other taxes	. . .	12	12
Property taxes	. . .	68	68
Payroll taxes	159	4	163
Total	489	227	716

Sources: Author's estimates based on data in *Survey of Current Business*, June 1982, pp. 6, 9. Figures are rounded.
a. Includes motor vehicle license tax and personal property tax.

Total taxes by source for 1980 are shown in table 2-3.[19] For all levels of government, personal taxes and payroll taxes on employers and employees amounted to almost two-thirds of the $716 billion in total taxes. However, as is well known, state and local governments rely much more heavily on indirect business taxes (which include property taxes) than does the federal government. For the lower levels of government, indirect business taxes accounted for 72 percent of total taxes paid by households; personal taxes (including payroll taxes) were equal to 24 percent; and 4 percent was derived from corporate profits taxes. For the federal government the distribution of revenue by source was quite different: 6 percent of total taxes paid by households can be attributed to indirect business taxes, 83 percent to personal income and payroll taxes, and 11 percent to the corporate profits tax.

19. Not all taxes paid by families are actually collected from the U.S. household population. A small portion of personal income taxes is collected from families living outside the United States, and some sales and other indirect business taxes are paid by foreigners on goods purchased in the United States. No adjustment was made for these taxes because the amounts involved are small.

Effective Tax Rates

Relative tax burdens are measured in this study by comparing effective rates of tax paid by family units. These are computed by expressing taxes paid as a percentage of income, and they thus reflect the proportion of the family's income that is accounted for by taxes. Although income is generally regarded as an acceptable measure, income for a single year (which may be unusually high or low) may be a poor indicator of "normal" financial status for many families. Current year income is used in this study for measuring tax burdens because income information for longer periods of time is not available.[20]

The income concept used for measuring effective tax rates is *not* family income as defined earlier in this chapter, but a concept derived from it called *adjusted family income*. This concept bears the same relationship to family income as net national product does to national income: adjusted family income is family income plus indirect business taxes. The relationship among the concepts of net national product, national income, family income, and adjusted family income is shown in table 2-4.[21]

Adjusted family income is the most appropriate income concept for comparing tax burdens because it would be incorrect to compare burdens that include sales and excise taxes with an income concept that does not include these taxes. Because tax burdens are being compared under several different shifting assumptions with reference to a proportional income tax, a consistent income basis must be used.[22] To achieve this, family income of all family units is increased proportionately by the ratio of indirect business taxes to family income, on the assumption that the use of indirect taxes does not alter

20. Tax burdens based on real incomes would also require information on the dates of purchase of assets, which is not available in any data source.

21. In addition to the adjustment for indirect business taxes, business transfer payments and the statistical discrepancy are subtracted from the net national product, and subsidies less the current surplus of government enterprises are added to arrive at national income.

22. For example, consider a country that produces total goods and services (net of depreciation) with a market price value of $1,000. Assume that it wants to levy $200 in taxes and is considering two alternatives. Under alternative A, half the tax revenue would be derived from sales taxes and half from an income tax, while under alternative B, all the revenue would come from an income tax. In both cases, the real effective tax rate is 20 percent. However, with alternative A, national income (valued at factor costs) is $900 (the $1,000 of net product less $100 of indirect business taxes paid by consumers), while with alternative B, the national income (which includes taxes levied on the earnings of factors of production) is the full $1,000. Thus unless indirect taxes are included in income, the tax burden would appear to be 22.2 percent under alternative A and 20 percent under alternative B.

Table 2-4. *Derivation of Net National Product, National Income,*
Family Income, and Adjusted Family Income, 1980
Billions of dollars

Description	Amount
Net national product	2,339
Minus: Indirect business tax accruals and other adjustments[a]	218
Equals: National income	2,121
Plus: Net adjustments to arrive at family income[b]	509
Equals: Family income as derived from the national income accounts	2,630
Plus: Indirect business taxes[c]	194
Equals: Adjusted family income	2,824

Sources: Author's estimates based on *Survey of Current Business*, June 1982, pp. 6, 9.
a. Includes business transfer payments, subsidies less current surplus of government enterprises, and the statistical discrepancy.
b. See table 2-1.
c. Excludes customs duties and nontax receipts and includes other adjustments required for the distribution of tax burdens to family units.

the distribution of factor incomes. The resulting concept is the basis for measuring effective rates of tax throughout this book.[23]

Measurement Procedures

In the past the income distribution data available for tax analysis have been deficient in two respects: they did not cover the entire income-receiving population, and they failed to include all the income known to have been received by those who were covered. Annual data on income subject to tax, based on individual tax returns, are available from the U.S. Internal Revenue Service, but because data for people not required to file returns are not included, the distribution for those at the low end of the income scale is distorted. The Bureau of the Census also collects income information in its

23. For an early discussion of this subject, see Tax Foundation, Inc., *The Tax Burden in Relation to National Income and Product*, Research Aid 4 (Tax Foundation, 1957). George A. Bishop examined the subject in detail in "Income Redistribution in the Framework of the National Income Accounts," *National Tax Journal*, vol. 19 (December 1966), and concluded that indirect taxes should be allocated on the basis of factor income. In a later study in which he participated, *Tax Burdens and Benefits of Government Expenditures by Income Class, 1961 and 1965* (Tax Foundation, 1967), indirect taxes were allocated on the basis of factor income—the basis used in this study—but the resulting income concept was not used to classify family units by income classes. The subject is also discussed by Richard A. Musgrave in *Theory of Public Finance* (McGraw-Hill, 1959), pp. 195–99; and, most recently, by Jacob P. Meerman, "The Definition of Income in Studies of Budget Incidence and Income Distribution," *Review of Income and Wealth*, Series 20, no. 4 (December 1974), pp. 515–22.

annual consumer survey (the Current Population Survey) each year from a representative sample of over 50,000 households. However, besides using a different population unit, the Census Bureau uses a *money income* concept—which includes transfer payments, such as social security and welfare benefits, but excludes capital gains. In addition, neither the Internal Revenue Service data nor the Census data contain any information on the distribution of nonmoney income and cannot be linked directly with the personal income or other aggregate statistics.

The Brookings MERGE Files

The lack of a consistent and comprehensive set of household income and tax data prompted the construction of new microanalytic data bases for use in this study—the MERGE files.[24] To create the files, information on the families included in the consumer surveys was matched with data from files containing information from federal individual income tax returns.[25] Thus the MERGE files contain data for low-income families, who are not in the tax-filing population, as well as the more complete—and more accurate—income tax information for higher-income families. In addition, income information in the MERGE files is corrected for nonreporting and underreporting, so that—with the appropriate weights applied to the sample units—the files account for the total income (on almost any desired definition of income) estimated to have been received in the United States.

Since the income-reporting units in the consumer surveys are samples of the entire U.S. population and the returns in the tax files are samples only of the tax-filing population, the final MERGE files are based on the demographic information for the families in the consumer files. But income data from the tax files were substituted for the corresponding information in the consumer files to take advantage of the superior income reporting on tax returns (including the information on capital gains that is excluded from the Census income concept). This was done first by estimating, on the basis of reported consumer information, the kind of tax return or returns that would

24. A detailed description of the methods used to create the MERGE files is given in Pechman and Okner, *Who Bears the Tax Burden?* app. A.

25. The consumer surveys used for this study were the 1967 Survey of Economic Opportunity for the 1966 file, the 1971 Consumer Population Survey for the 1970 file, and the 1975 Survey of Income and Education for the 1975 file. The 1966 and 1970 matches were prepared at Brookings. The match for the 1975 file was prepared by the Office of Tax Analysis, U.S. Treasury Department. The procedures described in the text were used to prepare the 1966 and 1970 file; the 1975 file was prepared in a similar, but not identical, fashion.

have been filed by members of each family and then, for tax filers, by matching each tax unit in the consumer surveys with returns selected from the tax files.

The ideal way to match the consumer data with the tax data would be to obtain the tax information directly from the Internal Revenue Service. This is not possible because neither the Census Bureau nor the Internal Revenue Service permits others to use their files with information identifying specific individuals or families. Instead of using an exact match, a means of simulating a match was developed. A return (or returns) "similar" to the return in the consumer survey was selected from the tax file, and income data from that record were substituted for the information in the consumer record. Because thousands of matches were made, the selection and linking of returns in the consumer surveys and tax files were done on a computer.

For most families, the MERGE files contain the demographic data and information on receipts of nontaxable income from the consumer files plus taxable income figures from the returns assigned to the family from the tax files. For consumer units deemed to be nonfilers, the MERGE files include no federal individual income tax information. Since there are very few high-income units in the consumer files, the upper portion of the tax files (representing less than 2 percent of the population) was substituted for the family units in the consumer survey.[26]

After substituting tax return data for the consumer income data, the total income not accounted for by the MERGE files amounted to about 10 percent of total family income. The next step was to adjust the data in the files to correspond with national aggregates. The aggregates for wages and salaries were usually very close, but there were significant discrepancies between expected and reported amounts of proprietor's income, interest, rent, and transfer payments. Some of the discrepancies were due to the partial coverage of the income concept used in the consumer surveys; the rest were due to nonreporting and underreporting of income by the survey respondents. Adjustments for these discrepancies were made on the basis of aggregates reported in other data sources, such as the national income accounts and the administrative records of federal agencies.[27]

In addition to adjustments for underreporting and nonreporting, income information was added to the MERGE files that is not available—because it is

26. The dividing line was the range where there was no obvious discontinuity in the number of family units when the tax file data were substituted for the consumer survey data.

27. For details see Pechman and Okner, *Who Bears the Tax Burden?* app. A.

not collected—in either the consumer surveys or the tax files. The information included rent on owner-occupied homes, employer supplements to wage and salary income, tax-exempt interest on state and local bonds, interest on life insurance policies, and accrued capital gains on farm assets and nonfarm real estate. These items were imputed on the basis of characteristics of the survey units in the MERGE file.[28]

Since no information on consumption was collected in the annual surveys, the final step in preparing the MERGE files was to estimate consumption for each family. This was done by extrapolation from the surveys of consumer expenditures conducted by the U.S. Bureau of Labor Statistics.[29] The consumption patterns (by item) were estimated on the basis of the age of family head, family size and composition, and the family's relative position in the income distribution.

Projections for 1980 and 1985

The methods described above were used to prepare original files for the years 1966, 1970, and 1975. To extend the analysis to more recent years, the 1975 file was projected to 1980 and 1985. The 1980 projections were based on the national income estimates for that year, and the 1985 projections were based on the projections in the president's budget for fiscal 1984.[30] Thus the 1966, 1970, and 1975 MERGE files are completely independent files, while those for 1980 and 1985 are derived from the 1975 file.

28. Thus, for example, accrued gains on capital assets are distributed among families on the basis of realized capital gains plus other property income reported on the returns in the tax file.

29. Consumption in the 1966 and 1970 MERGE files was estimated on the basis of the 1960–61 BLS survey; for the files for later years, the 1972–73 survey was used.

30. For the population projections see U.S. Bureau of the Census, "Projections of the Number of Households and Families: 1979 to 1985," *Current Population Reports*, Series P-25, no. 805 (May 1979). For the 1980 income estimates, see *Survey of Current Business*, June 1982, pp. 6, 9; for the 1985 projections see *Budget of the United States Government, Fiscal Year 1984*, pp. 2-9, 2-10. The weights for each sample unit were first increased to equal the population totals for 1980 and 1985. Then the projections were made by increasing each source of income for each sample unit in the 1975 file by the estimated percentage increase in the aggregate for that source from 1975 to 1980 or 1985. The tax calculations were based on the laws actually in effect in 1980 and on the laws scheduled for 1985 as of January 1, 1983.

CHAPTER THREE

Incidence Assumptions

PAST STUDIES of the distribution of tax burdens by income class have been based on a more or less standard set of assumptions about the incidence of the major taxes. The individual income tax was assumed to be borne by those who paid it; sales taxes and excises, by consumers of the taxed commodities; and corporation income tax, in part by stockholders and the remainder by consumers and occasionally corporate employees. The property tax on residences was regarded as a tax on housing services, and the tax on commercial and industrial buildings was assumed to be shifted to consumers. The property tax on land was allocated to owners of land. Payroll taxes imposed on employees were assumed to be borne by them, while those imposed on employers were assumed to be shifted partly to employees and partly to consumers.[1] These assumptions were pragmatic compromises made by analysts in the absence of a consensus among economists on the incidence of the major taxes in the tax system.

During the past twenty-five years there has been a substantial change in the method used by economists to analyze tax incidence.[2] The distinguishing

1. An early study along these lines was by Gerhard Colm and Helen Tarasov, *Who Pays the Taxes?* a study made for the Temporary National Economic Committee, Monograph 3, Investigation of Concentration of Economic Power, 76 Cong. 3 sess. (1940). The classic study is by R. A. Musgrave and others, "Distribution of Tax Payments by Income Groups: A Case Study for 1948," *National Tax Journal,* vol. 4 (March 1951). See also W. Irwin Gillespie, "Effect of Public Expenditures on the Distribution of Income," in Richard A. Musgrave, ed., *Essays in Fiscal Federalism* (Brookings, 1965); Roger A. Herriot and Herman P. Miller, "The Taxes We Pay," *Conference Board Record,* vol. 8 (May 1971); and Richard A. Musgrave and Peggy B. Musgrave, *Public Finance in Theory and Practice,* 4th ed. (McGraw-Hill, 1984), chap. 12. Only the Musgrave studies have provided estimates for alternative incidence assumptions.

2. Essential elements of the basic theory can be found in Harry Gunnison Brown, *The Economics of Taxation* (Holt, 1924), but his views had relatively little influence. The key roles in the more recent development were played by Musgrave, Rolph, and Harberger. See Richard A. Musgrave, *The Theory of Public Finance: A Study in Public Economy* (McGraw-Hill, 1959),

23

feature of this method is that it provides a consistent framework for the analysis of tax incidence, although it has not eliminated differences of opinion about the incidence of particular taxes. Nevertheless, important modifications have been made in the conclusions about the distribution of the burdens of some of the major taxes in the U.S. tax system.

This chapter summarizes the major elements of modern incidence theory, the conclusions that can be derived from it on the basis of alternative assumptions about the behavior of economic units, and the assumptions on which the calculations in this study are based. The study compares the distribution of tax burdens by income class under eight sets of assumptions, without making a choice among them. The objectives of the calculations are, first, to determine whether it is possible to arrive at any broad conclusions about the distribution of tax burdens in this country whatever the correct assumptions may be; and, second, to illustrate the differences implied by the major competing views among economists about the incidence of particular taxes. The calculations do not provide any empirical evidence either to verify or to deny the validity of competing incidence assumptions or the analysis based on any particular set of assumptions.

Incidence Theory[3]

The current approach attempts to determine the incidence of a tax by following through its effects on, first, the incomes received by the producers of the taxed commodity or sector (the sources of funds) and, second, the consumption expenditures of individual families (the uses of funds). The burden of a tax on any family is the sum of the burdens borne by its members both as producers and as consumers.

---

chap. 10; Earl R. Rolph, *The Theory of Fiscal Economics* (University of California Press, 1954); and Arnold C. Harberger, "The Incidence of the Corporation Income Tax," *Journal of Political Economy*, vol. 70 (June 1962). Mieszkowski and McLure have also made significant contributions to understanding the new theory. See Peter M. Mieszkowski, "On the Theory of Tax Incidence," *Journal of Political Economy*, vol. 75 (June 1967); and Charles E. McLure, Jr., "Tax Incidence, Macroeconomic Policy, and Absolute Prices," *Quarterly Journal of Economics*, vol. 84 (May 1970), and "General Equilibrium Incidence Analysis: The Harberger Model After Ten Years," *Journal of Public Economics*, vol. 4 (February 1975).

3. This section may be omitted by readers who are interested primarily in the statement of the incidence assumptions used in this study. Those readers are referred to the next major section in this chapter.

Outline of Current Theory

The incidence of a tax depends on its impact on relative prices and relative factor incomes. Through its monetary and fiscal policies the government can cause the general price level to rise, fall, or remain unchanged when a tax is increased or a new tax is imposed. Consequently the absolute price level is not relevant to incidence analysis. What is relevant is the effect of a tax on the distribution of *real* incomes that are available for private use; and this depends on the changes in relative product and factor prices and not on changes in absolute prices.[4] So as not to confuse the incidence of a tax change with the effect of fiscal and monetary policies on total output, full employment is assumed to exist before and after a tax is introduced or changed.

The analysis assumes perfect competition, price flexibility, and perfect factor mobility. It also assumes that factors receive the value of their marginal products. While these assumptions may not hold for the short run, they may be reasonable for the longer run when adjustments to changes in relative output prices may be expected to take place.

The effect of changes in the returns to labor and capital has been the subject of considerable empirical research in recent years.[5] Efforts have also been made to construct general equilibrium models incorporating taxpayer responses to taxes.[6] However, this research has not developed sufficiently to be incorporated into the analysis of tax incidence at the family level. Thus for purposes of this study the supplies of labor and saving are assumed to be relatively inelastic with respect to changes in factor returns and therefore are taken to be fixed even in the long run.

A tax will raise the price of the taxed product or factor relative to the prices of products or factors that are not taxed or are taxed at lower rates. Consequently, producers will tend to use less of a factor of production that is taxed more heavily; and consumers will tend to consume less of a commodity that is taxed more heavily. As a result of these relative price changes, a tax may cause a substantial shift of labor and capital among industries and in the

4. See Musgrave, *Theory of Public Finance*, pp. 364–65; McLure, "Tax Incidence"; and John A. Brittain, *The Payroll Tax for Social Security* (Brookings, 1972), pp. 32–36, 53–55.

5. See, for example, Lawrence H. Summers, "Capital Taxation and Accumulation in a Life Cycle Growth Model," *American Economic Review*, vol. 71 (September 1981); and Jerry Hausman, "Labor Supply," in Henry J. Aaron and Joseph A. Pechman, eds., *How Taxes Affect Economic Behavior* (Brookings, 1981).

6. See John B. Shoven, "Applied General-Equilibrium Tax Modeling," International Monetary Fund *Staff Papers*, vol. 30 (June 1983); and John B. Shoven and John Whalley, "Applied General-Equilibrium Models of Taxation and International Trade," *Journal of Economic Literature*, vol. 22 (1984).

consumption patterns of families.[7] These allocative effects may reduce consumer satisfaction with particular commodities, but they are disregarded in the analysis here, both because they are believed to be small relative to the total burden of most taxes and because they cannot be measured. What is left is the change in incomes earned by factors of production that results from the tax change and the change in the purchasing power of these incomes from the shifts in relative prices of consumer goods and services.[8]

Even if relative factor and product prices were changed by the imposition of a tax, there would be no change in relative real incomes if all families derived their incomes from the same sources and in the same proportions, and if their expenditure patterns were the same. In such cases, the burden of every tax would be proportional to income. The incidence question arises because changes in relative factor and product prices affect families at different income levels to different degrees.[9] However, often the uses side of income can be ignored because the expenditure patterns of those who are affected by the tax are similar,[10] or the sources-of-income side can be ignored because relative factor prices do not change.[11]

One of the major issues in incidence analysis is how to account for the uses of tax funds by the government. Clearly, relative factor earnings and product prices in the private economy may be altered as much by the way government spends its revenues as by the way it raises them. To avoid the need to trace through the effects of government expenditures as well as taxes on private incomes, some economists make the unrealistic assumption that the government spends the tax proceeds in the same way the money would have been

7. A tax may also increase or reduce the nonmarket activities of persons in households. For example, a tax on money income or money consumption may encourage individuals to work less or spend less on goods offered in the marketplace and consume more leisure.

8. Since it is assumed that the government follows a full-employment policy, the tax will not reduce total income because its deflationary effect will be offset by appropriate fiscal and monetary policies. The imposition of a tax is sometimes followed by increased unemployment, but this is the result of poor government policy and should not be attributed to the tax itself.

9. Inferences about the incidence of a tax cannot be based on changes in relative factor or product prices alone. Incidence depends also on the elasticities of demand for the taxed and untaxed commodities, elasticities of substitution between capital and labor, initial factor shares, and marginal propensities to consume.

10. For example, as will be noted below (note 46), there is little reason to believe that there is a disproportionate consumption of labor-intensive products and services at one end of the income scale or of capital-intensive products and services at the other end. Hence the burden on family budgets of a general tax on labor or capital can be ignored.

11. Relative factor prices are unlikely to be changed by a general consumption tax or value added tax or when factor proportions in different industries are the same.

spent by the taxpayers.[12] Others assume, more realistically, that substituting government spending for private spending does not significantly alter relative factor prices or the relative prices paid by consumers.[13] Still others address the problem by comparing the effects of two or more sets of taxes with the same yield. By assuming that government expenditures would be the same with either tax or set of taxes, the complication that is brought about by different patterns of government spending is avoided.[14]

This study is based on the differential incidence approach, using a proportional income tax as the basis for comparison. The question the differential approach attempts to answer is, how does the distribution of disposable incomes of households under the present tax system differ from what it would be if the federal, state, and local government taxes they pay were collected through a proportional income tax with the same yield?[15] Each tax in the tax system is analyzed in this way, and the results are added together to arrive at the distributional impact of the entire tax system. The aggregate burdens are equal to the sum of the burdens of the individual taxes because each tax is compared with the same tax—a proportional income tax—with equal yield.[16]

Implications of the Theory

The competitive model suggests the following conclusions about the incidence of the major taxes in the U.S. tax system:

1. The *individual income tax* probably is not shifted if workers and investors do not change hours worked or saving in response to changes in tax rates. Among all groups in the labor force there is evidence that labor force participation or hours of work may be affected by the income tax mainly in the

12. See, for example, Harberger, "Incidence of the Corporation Income Tax," p. 224.

13. For example, it is probably true that the expenditures of social security recipients are not very different from the expenditures forgone by those who pay the payroll taxes that finance social security benefits. See Brittain, *Payroll Tax for Social Security,* p. 50.

14. However, this assumption involves other difficulties. In the first place, it takes for granted that the marginal effect of the two taxes on the consumption of taxpayers with different liabilities under alternative tax systems is the same. Second, the *monetary* yield required to purchase the same assortment of goods and services may change if relative prices are affected by the tax change. See Musgrave, *Theory of Public Finance,* pp. 211–17.

15. The reference tax is a proportional income tax that would apply, with no exemptions and deductions, to adjusted family income, as defined in chapter 2.

16. This technique was first used by Musgrave and others in "Distribution of Tax Payments by Income Groups," pp. 5–8, 37–39. For a more recent application of the technique, see Richard A. Musgrave, Karl E. Case, and Herman Leonard, "The Distribution of Fiscal Burdens and Benefits," *Public Finance Quarterly,* vol. 2 (July 1974).

case of young people and some women, but the effect on total labor supplied is small.[17] The private saving rate when the economy is operating at or near full employment has been constant for many years, despite large changes in the total tax burden and in its composition.[18] If total hours worked and saving are relatively fixed, a tax on incomes is borne by those on whom the tax is imposed. This is based on the presumption that imposing the tax does not change either the demand for, or the supply of, factors of production (because productivity is not altered by the tax) and that factor proportions thus remain unchanged. There is therefore no reason why purchasers should pay more for the same amount of capital or labor after a tax is imposed than before. Since the tax does not change relative product prices, there is no burden on the uses side of household budgets.[19]

  2. A *general sales tax* is borne by consumers in proportion to their total expenditures because the tax does not change relative prices and hence does not alter consumption patterns.[20] Excise taxes do change relative prices, thus

  17. For a review of the literature, see Barry P. Bosworth, *Tax Incentives and Economic Growth* (Brookings, 1984), pp. 133–44. Relatively large effects on labor supply have been obtained by Jerry A. Hausman in "Labor Supply." If Hausman's estimates are corroborated by further research, the incidence effects of individual income and payroll taxes presented in this volume would have to be modified.

  18. See Edward F. Denison, "A Note on Private Saving," *Review of Economics and Statistics,* vol. 40 (August 1958); and Paul A. David and John L. Scadding, "Private Savings: Ultrarationality, Aggregation, and 'Denison's Law,' " *Journal of Political Economy,* vol. 82 (March–April, 1974). Warren E. Weber, in "The Effect of Interest Rates on Aggregate Consumption," *American Economic Review,* vol. 60 (September 1970), found that increases in interest rates *reduce* consumer saving. On the other hand, Colin Wright, "Saving and the Rate of Interest," in Arnold C. Harberger and Martin J. Bailey, eds., *The Taxation of Income from Capital* (Brookings, 1969), pp. 275–300, found that the interest elasticity of consumer saving ranges from 0.18 to 0.27. Michael J. Boskin has the highest estimate (0.4), "Taxation, Saving, and the Rate of Interest," *Journal of Political Economy,* vol. 86 (April 1978), pt. 2; but E. Philip Howrey and Saul H. Hymans found that the elasticity was close to zero, "The Measurement and Determination of Loanable-Funds Saving," *Brookings Papers on Economic Activity 3:1978.* No one has estimated the effect of interest rates on total private saving.

  19. A progressive tax would reduce the demand for commodities consumed by the highest income groups relative to that for commodities consumed by lower income groups. This same type of change in spending patterns occurs as a result of the imposition of special excise taxes. As was noted above in this chapter, the effect of such changes is not taken into account in this analysis.

  20. If all income were consumed, the incidence of a general consumption tax and that of a proportional income tax would be identical. In such a case, the two taxes would be borne in proportion to the initial shares of each household in total income, and it would be meaningless to try to distinguish between burdens on the sources and those on the uses of income. If some income is saved, the incidence of the two taxes becomes distinct; the proportional income tax is then borne in proportion to income (the sources side), while the general consumption tax is borne

burdening those who consume the commodities that are subject to tax. There is no burden on the sources-of-income side, however, because any labor or capital that may shift from the taxed industries ultimately receives approximately the same income when it is reemployed in the untaxed industries.[21]

3. The *corporation income tax* depresses rates of return in the corporate sector when it is imposed. This encourages some capital to move to the noncorporate sector, where rates of return after tax are initially higher. As the supply of capital in the noncorporate sector increases, rates of return decline there, and this continues until net returns after tax are the same in both sectors. Thus the after-tax rates of return on all capital are reduced even though the corporation income tax is imposed only on capital employed in the corporate sector.[22] Furthermore, assuming that the total supply of saving is fixed, the earnings of labor remain unchanged, and capital bears the entire tax. The effect of the corporation income tax on the uses of income is ignored because there is no evidence that consumers in one income class spend proportionately more or less of their income on corporate products than do consumers in other income classes.[23]

4. Since the supply of land is fixed, the *property tax on land* is borne by landowners when the tax is first levied or increased.[24] The *property tax on*

---

in proportion to consumption (the uses side). See Mieszkowski, "On the Theory of Tax Incidence," p. 251.

21. Browning and Johnson assume that households consume approximately the same proportion of their income when longer time periods than a year are considered. Consequently, consumption taxes impose no differential tax burdens on the sources side of income. Moreover, since most transfer payments are indexed, they argue that recipients of transfers do not bear any of the burden of consumption taxes. Accordingly, they allocate the burden of all consumption taxes to factor incomes. See Edgar K. Browning and William R. Johnson, *The Distribution of the Tax Burden* (American Enterprise Institute, 1979), chap. 2.

22. On the assumption that the total supply of saving in the economy as a whole is not affected by the after-tax rate of return, the before-tax rate of return for the economy as a whole is unchanged by the tax even though the before-tax rate of return in the corporate sector is, in the end, higher than that in the noncorporate sector.

23. If saving is responsive to the rate of return on capital, the corporation income tax may be shifted in part to labor in the long run. See Martin Feldstein, "Tax Incidence in a Growing Economy with Variable Factor Supply," *Quarterly Journal of Economics,* vol. 88 (November 1974); Boskin, "Taxation, Saving, and the Rate of Interest"; and Summers, "Capital Taxation and Accumulation in a Life Cycle Growth Model."

24. As was explained above, when the supply of a particular factor is fixed, the owners of the factor must bear the tax. However, if the supply of land is variable, a land tax would increase the price of land, and consumers would bear at least part of the tax. See Peter Mieszkowski, "The Property Tax: An Excise Tax or a Profits Tax?" *Journal of Public Economics,* vol. 1 (April 1972).

buildings has approximately the same effect that the corporation income tax has on the sources of income.[25] If the total supply of saving (and therefore of investment) is not responsive to the rate of return, a partial or a general property tax on buildings is shifted to the owners of capital in general in the form of lower rates of return in a manner exactly parallel to that of the corporate tax.[26] On the uses side, the property tax raises the price of housing services and other goods and services produced in buildings, relative to other prices.[27] Since the proportion of total income spent on housing falls when income rises (with income measured on an annual basis), this would suggest that the burden of the property tax falls as family income rises. However, the elasticity of housing expenditures with respect to income is higher when families are classified on the basis of incomes over a period of years rather than one year.[28] Furthermore, the difference among income levels in the impact of relative price changes is probably small even if the elasticity with respect to permanent income is less than 1.0—partly because there is evidence that the ratio of the value of capital to rental prices increases as rents increase and partly because the property tax on commercial and industrial buildings is also reflected in the relative prices of goods consumed by families in the higher income classes.

25. This is true only of a uniform property tax. Since the property tax varies greatly among (and within) communities, the property tax has differential effects similar to those of variable excise taxes. (See Mieszkowski, "The Property Tax.") In this study, only the *average* property tax is allocated by income classes; the effects of property taxes that depart from the average are ignored.

26. Like the corporation income tax, the property tax on buildings may well be shifted in part to labor if saving is elastic with respect to the rate of return in the long run. See Feldstein, "Tax Incidence in a Growing Economy with Variable Factor Supply"; and Boskin, "Taxation, Saving, and the Rate of Interest."

27. If the property tax were perfectly general and the supply of saving were not responsive to the rate of return, the price of housing services would not rise relative to the price of other goods and services. However, the property tax on improvements is generally confined to buildings (it applies to equipment and inventories in only a few states), and thus it is not a general tax on capital in actual application. If it were a general capital tax, it would impose no differential burden on the uses side.

28. The elasticity of expenditure for housing with respect to permanent income is in dispute. According to de Leeuw and Aaron, housing expenditures are roughly proportional to permanent income (that is, they have an elasticity of about 1.0). See Frank de Leeuw, "The Demand for Housing: A Review of Cross-Section Evidence," *Review of Economics and Statistics*, vol. 53 (February 1971); and Henry J. Aaron, *Shelter and Subsidies: Who Benefits from Federal Housing Policies?* (Brookings, 1972), pp. 212–13. However, estimates by Carliner, based on a panel of households over a four-year period, suggest that the elasticity is about 0.6–0.7 for owners and 0.5 for renters. See Geoffrey Carliner, "Income Elasticity of Housing Demand," *Review of Economics and Statistics*, vol. 55 (November 1973), p. 531.

5. Like the individual income tax, the *payroll tax* is assumed to be borne by workers because lower take-home pay as a result of the tax will not induce wage earners to withdraw from the labor force. In these circumstances, the same number of workers will be seeking the same number of jobs. Since workers are no more productive as a result of the imposition of the tax, employers have no reason to pay higher total compensation. With before-tax compensation the same, the payroll tax is borne by workers.[29] This reasoning applies to payroll taxes levied on employers as well as to those levied on employees.[30]

Effects of Changing Assumptions

Although the framework of the above analysis is accepted by many economists, there is some skepticism about the conclusions, on the ground that the assumptions on which they are based are unrealistic.[31] Markets are not perfectly competitive, and labor and capital are not necessarily mobile, even in the long run. Moreover, many economists do not accept the proposition that taxation has little effect on the supply of saving or on work effort. They contend that, on the basis of other assumptions, which they regard as more realistic, the results of this analysis must be modified—at least in the case of the corporation income tax, the property tax, and the employer payroll tax.[32]

• With regard to the *corporation income tax,* it is argued that there is no evidence that unincorporated business in the United States has grown at the expense of corporate business in response to increases in corporate taxes. The corporate share of the national income originating in business enterprises rose—with only temporary interruptions—from 58 percent in 1929 to 75 per-

---

29. Even if labor responded to the payroll tax by working fewer hours or by withdrawing from the labor force, labor would not necessarily be able to shift the tax. Although wage rates might increase in these circumstances, employment would probably be reduced; and, under plausible assumptions concerning the elasticity of demand for labor, the aggregate wage bill would be reduced by at least as much as the tax proceeds. See Brittain, *The Payroll Tax for Social Security,* pp. 39–44, 55–57.

30. Most public finance experts believe that the economic effects of a payroll tax are the same whether it is levied on employers or employees (see, for example, Musgrave and Musgrave, *Public Finance in Theory and Practice,* p. 496). For an empirical verification that payroll taxes are borne by employees even when the tax is levied on employers, see Brittain, *Payroll Tax for Social Security,* pp. 59, 60–81.

31. The implications of this view are discussed by Musgrave and Musgrave in *Public Finance in Theory and Practice,* chap. 12.

32. It should be reemphasized that the author does not necessarily agree with these assumptions or those discussed earlier, or with the implications drawn from them.

cent in 1982.[33] Much of the increase came from the relative decline of farm-
ing, in which corporations are not important. But even in the rest of the
economy there is no indication that corporate output has been reduced as a
result of the post–World War II rates of corporate taxation. If capital does not
move from the corporate to the noncorporate sector in response to the tax, the
burden of the tax will fall entirely on the owners of corporate capital.[34] The
national income accounts treat the corporation income tax as a direct tax on
corporations and thus are consistent with the view that the tax is not shifted.[35]

Yet a different result is obtained if one believes that the corporation income
tax affects corporate pricing and output decisions. The classical view is that
the corporation income tax is not shifted in the short run, whether business
firms operate in competitive or in monopolistic markets.[36] The reasoning is as
follows: maximum profits occur when the cost of producing an additional unit
of output is equal to the additional revenue obtained from selling it. Assuming
that the firm seeks to maximize its net profit, the level of output and prices
that maximized profits before the tax was imposed will still maximize profits
after the tax is imposed. Consequently, a corporation income tax should have
no effect on pricing decisions.

The argument against this view is that today's markets are neither perfectly
competitive nor perfectly monopolistic and that firms do not necessarily seek
to maximize their profits. In such markets, business firms have the power to
set their prices to cover what they regard as costs plus a margin for profits.
The firms may treat the corporation income tax as an element of cost and raise
their prices sufficiently to recover the tax. Alternatively the firms may have a
target rate of return on invested capital. If this rate of return is to be preserved
after a tax is imposed, the tax must be shifted forward to consumers or
backward to workers; or it may be shifted partly forward and partly backward.[37] Still another possibility is that the leading firms in an industry may

33. See Joseph A. Pechman, *Federal Tax Policy,* 4th ed. (Brookings, 1983), p. 138.
34. This assumes that the total supply of savings remains unchanged. See note 23.
35. For the treatment of the corporation income tax in the national income accounts, see U.S.
Department of Commerce, Bureau of Economic Analysis, *The National Income and Product
Accounts of the United States, 1929–76 Statistical Tables* (U.S. Government Printing Office,
1981).
36. The "short run" is a period that is too short for firms to adjust their capital to changing
demand and supply conditions. The "long run" is a period in which the stock of capital can be
adjusted.
37. See Marian Krzyzaniak and Richard A. Musgrave, *The Shifting of the Corporation
Income Tax* (Johns Hopkins Press, 1963), pp. 1–3. This view has been vigorously debated among
economists. For the opposing view, see Richard E. Slitor, "Corporate Tax Incidence: Economic
Adjustments to Differentials under a Two-Tier Tax Structure," and Richard Goode, "Rates of

raise their prices to recover the tax and the tax will merely form an "umbrella" that permits less efficient or marginal producers to survive.[38]

• The *property tax on buildings* could also be shifted to consumers in the form of higher prices in the same way that the corporation tax might be shifted; that is, to the extent that property owners do not try to maximize their profits and have sufficient market power, they may be able to increase rents when a property tax is imposed. Furthermore, doubts arise about the incidence of the property tax if saving is responsive to rates of return. In these circumstances the initial effect of imposing a property tax is to reduce the rates of return to owners of real estate; but this reduction will ultimately discourage new investment and reduce the supply of buildings. The result will be a rise in the prices of services that are produced by dwelling units. Thus, instead of resting on the owners of real estate, the burden of the property tax on residential buildings will be shifted to tenants. Owner-occupants, who in effect are renters of their own homes, will also bear the residential property tax, but as consumers of housing services and not as owners of dwelling units.[39] Similarly the burden of the property tax on other buildings will not fall on their owners, but will be shifted to consumers in general. These assumptions are incorporated in the national income accounts, which treat state-local real estate taxes as indirect business taxes.[40]

• The proposition that the burden of the *property tax on unimproved land* falls on the owner when the tax is imposed or increased has been accepted by virtually every economist since Ricardo.[41] But even this proposition is being

Return, Income Shares, and Corporate Tax Incidence," both in Marian Krzyzaniak, ed., *Effects of Corporation Income Tax* (Wayne State University Press, 1966); and John G. Cragg, Arnold C. Harberger, and Peter Mieszkowski, "Empirical Evidence on the Incidence of the Corporation Income Tax," *Journal of Political Economy,* vol. 75 (December 1967), pp. 811–21 (Brookings Reprint 146). For a continuation of the debate, see Marian Krzyzaniak and Richard A. Musgrave, "Corporation Tax Shifting: A Response," *Journal of Political Economy,* vol. 78 (July–August 1970), pp. 768–73; and in the same journal, Cragg, Harberger, and Mieszkowski, "Corporation Tax Shifting: Rejoinder," pp. 747–77.

38. Committee for Economic Development, *Tax Reduction and Tax Reform: When and How* (New York: CED, May 1957), pp. 24–25.

39. See Dick Netzer, *Economics of the Property Tax* (Brookings, 1966), p. 36. The entire tax can be shifted in the form of higher prices in these circumstances only if the demand for housing services is perfectly inelastic or the supply of housing is perfectly elastic (that is, if housing can be produced at constant costs).

40. The tax on land is also included in indirect business tax accruals in the accounts, but this decision was apparently based on the fact that the available data do not separate the tax on land from the tax on other real estate—rather than on the assumption that the tax is shifted.

41. See David Ricardo, *On the Principles of Political Economy and Taxation,* vol. 1 of Piero Sraffa, ed., *The Works and Correspondence of David Ricardo* (Cambridge University Press, 1951), chap. 10.

challenged by some economists who argue that, when a property tax is imposed on land and on reproducible capital simultaneously, investors who would otherwise have purchased land cannot obtain a higher rate of return by putting their funds to other uses. Hence, according to this view, a general property tax reduces the rates of return on all assets[42] and, like the corporation income tax, is borne by owners of capital in general.

• The conclusion that the *payroll tax* burden falls on wage earners is disputed by economists who do not accept the economic model on which that conclusion is based. According to the alternative view, it is unrealistic to assume perfectly rational behavior in labor markets and to take no account of the possible effect of collective bargaining agreements between large firms and large labor unions. Labor unions may succeed in inducing management to raise gross wages when a payroll tax is imposed or increased. If the firms have enough market power, they may be able to raise prices and thus shift at least part of the payroll tax to consumers. The share of labor in total national income will remain unchanged, but the prices of labor-intensive goods and services will rise relative to others.

Assumptions Used in This Study

The eight sets of assumptions used in the calculations in this study may be classified into three basic variants, each illustrating a major approach to incidence. The assumptions in each group were chosen to illustrate the effect of modifications in the incidence of one or more of the major taxes.[43] In all eight sets it is assumed that the individual income tax is not shifted by the taxpayer and that general sales and excise taxes are borne by consumers in proportion to their consumption of the taxed items. The differences among the

42. Assume that the rate of interest is 10 percent and a tax of 1 percent is imposed on all capital. If a parcel of land was worth $100 before the tax was imposed, it yielded a rent of $10 a year. The tax will reduce the after-tax rent from $10 to $9; but, since the tax is general, the interest rate will fall from 10 percent to 9 percent, and the value of the land will remain unchanged at $100. Thus the land tax is not capitalized and is paid out of rents. Another way of reaching the same conclusion is that differential land taxes affect the relative price of land in various jurisdictions. The imposition of a distortionary tax on land in one jurisdiction leads to a reallocation of (mobile) capital throughout the nation and reduces the after-tax return to capital by the amount of tax collected by the taxing jurisdiction. See Peter Mieszkowski and George R. Zodrow, "The Incidence of the Local Property Tax: A Reevaluation," Working Paper 1485 (National Bureau of Economic Research, October 1984).

43. In some cases the modifications are not strictly consistent with the basic rationale of the particular group of variants.

Table 3-1. *Tax Incidence Assumptions Used in This Study*[a]

Tax and basis of allocation	Variant 1			Variant 2		Variant 3		
	a	*b*	*c*	*a*	*b*	*a*	*b*	*c*
Individual income tax								
To taxpayers	X	X	X	X	X	X	X	X
Sales and excise taxes								
To consumption of taxed commodities	X	X	X	X	X	X	X	X
Corporation income tax								
To dividends	...	...	...	X	X	...	...	...
To property income in general	X	X	...	...	...	...	...	...
Half to dividends, half to property income in general	...	...	X	...	...	...	...	X
Half to dividends, one-fourth to consumption, one-fourth to employee compensation	...	...	...	...	...	X	...	...
Half to property income in general, half to consumption	...	...	...	...	...	...	X	...
Property tax on land								
To landowners	X	...	...	X	X	X	X	X
To property income in general	...	X	X	...	...	...	...	...
Property tax on improvements								
To shelter and consumption	...	...	...	X	X	X	X	...
To property income in general	X	X	X	...	...	...	...	...
Half to shelter and consumption, half to property income in general	...	...	...	...	...	...	...	X
Payroll tax on employees								
To employee compensation	X	X	X	X	X	X	X	X
Payroll tax on employers								
To employee compensation	X	X	X	X	...	X	...	X
Half to employee compensation, half to consumption	...	...	...	...	X	...	X	...

a. See text for a detailed description of the incidence variants.

sets relate to the incidence of the corporation, property, and payroll taxes.[44] The variants and modifications are summarized in table 3-1 and are described briefly below.

Variant 1 illustrates the distribution of tax burdens if the supplies of labor

44. The Browning-Johnson assumption that consumption taxes are borne in proportion to factor income (see note 21) is not included in the variants of this study. The effect of this assumption would be to make the distribution of tax burden more progressive than any of the

and capital are assumed to be fixed and there is perfect competition, price flexibility, and perfect factor mobility. Payroll taxes on both employers and employees are assumed to be borne by employees in proportion to their taxed earnings; the corporation income tax and the property tax on improvements are regarded as taxes on all property income and are distributed in proportion to the property income reported by each household. In variant 1a it is assumed further that the property tax on land is capitalized and is therefore borne by landowners in proportion to the value of land owned.[45] In variants 1b and 1c, the property tax on land is treated in the same way as the property tax on improvements (that is, it is allocated to property income in general). In addition, in variant 1c half the corporation income tax is assumed to be borne by stockholders and the other half by owners of property in general.

In *variant 2* the corporation income tax is allocated to stockholders in proportion to the dividends they received; the property tax on dwellings is allocated in proportion to the cash or imputed rent of households; and the property tax on commercial and industrial real estate is allocated to consumption in general. The two sets of assumptions in this variant differ in the treatment of the payroll tax levied on employers. In variant 2a, which follows the assumptions implicit in the national income accounts, the employer payroll tax is assumed to be borne by employees. In variant 2b half of the employer tax is assumed to be shifted to consumers and the other half to be paid by employees.[46]

Variant 3 presents several compromises among the views on tax incidence represented in the other variants. Variant 3a allocates the corporation income tax among three groups: half to stockholders, one-fourth to consumers of

---

incidence variants used in this study. On the other hand, the Feldstein-Boskin view that taxes on property income reduce investment and ultimately total output (see note 23) would make the tax system more regressive because such taxes would then be borne to a large extent by labor. Similarly, the Hausman view that individual income taxes reduce labor supply (see note 17) leads to the conclusion that such taxes may be borne in part by capital through a reduction in total output. Readers who want to see what effect these and other assumptions would have on tax burdens can substitute for the distributions of taxes used in this study the relative burdens based on their own assumptions. The data for making these calculations are available on request.

45. Under this assumption the present property tax was borne by the landowners when the property tax was first imposed and by those who were the owners when the tax was increased. Since these owners cannot now be identified, the property tax is allocated in this study to present landowners because they are the ones who would benefit from its removal.

46. Strictly speaking, if the employer tax is shifted, the tax is borne by consumers of labor-intensive goods and services. However, information on the consumption of labor-intensive goods relative to that of capital-intensive goods by income classes is not available. Accordingly, in this variant the employer tax is allocated on the basis of total consumption.

corporate products, and the remaining one-fourth to corporate employees. In all other respects, this variant follows the national income accounts assumptions (variant 2a). In variant 3b half the corporation income tax is allocated to consumers and the remaining half is allocated to property income in general; in addition, half the payroll tax on employers is assumed to be shifted to consumers. In variant 3c half the corporation income tax is borne by stockholders and half by property-income recipients in general; the payroll tax is assumed to be borne entirely by employees; and half of the property tax on improvements is assumed to be borne by recipients of property income and the other half to be shifted in the form of higher prices for shelter and consumption goods.

As already noted in chapter 1, the analysis in this volume is confined to the distribution of tax burdens, without reference to the benefits supported by taxes. Since payroll taxes in the U.S. tax system are earmarked to pay for social insurance programs, it can be argued that the distribution of tax burdens alone is incomplete. For this reason, incomes before and after transfer payments as well as taxes for the year 1980 is shown in chapter 4, and the effect of each on the distribution of income is given in figure 1-2.

Relation between Income and Taxes

Although it is not immediately obvious, the total amount of income of units in the household sector, as well as the taxes paid by them, depends on the incidence assumptions for the various taxes. Under the practice followed in the national income accounts, taxes borne by labor or capital are included in the national income computed at factor costs. Indirect business tax accruals, which are assumed to be shifted to consumers, are included in the national income computed at market prices.[47] As was indicated in chapter 2, *family income,* as the term is used in this study, corresponds to the national income at factor costs, while *adjusted family income* corresponds to national income at market prices.

However, these relations apply only under the incidence assumptions used in the national income accounts (variant 2a). Whenever there is a departure from these assumptions—that is, when a tax is assumed to be borne by consumers rather than by labor or capital, or vice versa—family incomes and adjusted family incomes must be modified. The modifications are required for

47. This is called *net national product* in the national income accounts.

two reasons: first, factor incomes are overstated in the national income accounts to the extent that the tax is shifted to consumers; and second, where
taxes are borne by property owners, the amount of taxes allocated to the
household sector will depend upon the proportion of total property income
received by that sector.[48]

Since all eight sets of assumptions in table 3-1 treat the individual income
tax and sales and excise taxes in the same way, modifications in family
income and in adjusted family income are needed to maintain consistency in
the definitions of "income" and "taxes" only in the cases of the corporation
income tax, the property tax, and the payroll tax.

• When the *corporation tax* is assumed to be borne entirely by stockholders, the tax is included in factor incomes and hence in family income. This is
the procedure used in the national income accounts. However, if part or all of
the corporation income tax is assumed to be borne by recipients of property
income in general, that part must be subtracted from incomes obtained from
the corporate sector and added to all property incomes. Similarly, if part or all
of the corporation tax is assumed to be shifted forward to consumers, that part
must be excluded from corporate incomes and added to indirect business
taxes.

• In the national income accounts, the *property tax* is regarded as an
indirect business tax. If all or part of the tax is regarded as a tax on property
incomes, property incomes as measured in the national income accounts must
be "grossed up" by the portion of the property tax that was not in factor
incomes.

• *Employer and employee payroll taxes* are treated in the national income
accounts as if both were borne by employees. If part or all of the payroll tax is
assumed to be shifted to consumers, that part should be deducted from employee compensation and treated as an indirect business tax.

When a tax on labor or capital is assumed to be shifted forward to consumers, the amount of family income (as defined in this study) is reduced, but
adjusted family income remains unchanged. However, in some cases the
population affected by the tax is different under the two sets of assumptions.
For example, if the corporation income tax is a tax on stockholders, the tax is
allocated between financial institutions and stockholders in the household
sector, and only the tax borne by individuals is included in family income. On
the other hand, if part of the corporation income tax is assumed to be shifted

---

48. In these adjustments it is assumed that consumption patterns and factor shares are the
same under the different incidence assumptions.

to consumers, that part is borne entirely by units of the household sector (since financial institutions do not make consumption expenditures). In this case, the shifted portion of the corporation income tax is excluded from family income, but it reappears as an indirect business tax in adjusted family income. In all cases, reductions and increases in family income are allocated among households in proportion to the income sources that are affected by the change. When a tax is distributed in proportion to property incomes in general, the allocation is made on the basis of property incomes *after* tax.

Table 3-2 summarizes the amounts of family income, adjusted family income, and taxes for each of the eight variants shown in table 3-1. Although there are significant differences in family income among the variants, differences in adjusted family income—which reflect only the differences in the populations to which taxes were allocated—are relatively small. As a result, the differences in effective tax rates are small, ranging from a low of 25.3 percent (variants 1b and 2b) to a high of 25.8 percent (variant 3b).

While the differences in aggregate effective rates are small, the tax burdens of individual families may vary greatly under the several sets of incidence assumptions. All income and tax adjustments are carried through to individual family units, and the distributions by income class reflect these adjustments. Therefore a family with an annual income of $10,000 under one set of assumptions may be classified in a higher income class under another set and in a lower class under a third set. Families are also reclassified on the basis of the relevant adjusted family incomes in the relative income (percentile) distributions. Consequently, in examining effective tax rates for any income class under the several incidence variants, it should be noted that the income classification (whether on an absolute or on a relative basis) does not necessarily contain the same families under each variant.

Allocation of Taxes by Income Class

Estimates of the taxes paid by each family unit in the MERGE files were made for each set of assumptions.[49] The federal individual income tax was

---

49. For details of the methods used to estimate taxes for each unit, see Pechman and Okner, *Who Bears the Tax Burden?* app. B. No attempt was made to estimate the "implicit" taxes in the form of reduced before-tax yields on assets eligible for tax preferences. For a discussion of this issue, see Harvey Galper and Eric Toder, "Transfer Elements in the Taxation of Income from Capital," Marilyn Moon, ed., *Economic Transfers in the United States* (University of Chicago Press, 1984).

Table 3-2. *Family Income, Adjusted Family Income, Taxes, and Effective Tax Rate under Various Incidence Assumptions, 1980*

Billions of dollars unless otherwise specified

Incidence variant[a]	Family income	Adjusted family income	Total taxes	Effective tax rate (percent)[b]
1a	2,702	2,829	720	25.5
1b	2,699	2,825	716	25.3
1c	2,694	2,820	711	25.5
2a	2,654	2,823	716	25.4
2b	2,609	2,823	716	25.3
3a	2,644	2,834	727	25.7
3b	2,583	2,839	732	25.8
3c	2,678	2,826	718	25.4

Source: 1980 Brookings MERGE file.

Note: Income and tax amounts are derived from aggregate control data and vary slightly from the effective rates in the MERGE file shown in tables 4-3 and 4-4.

a. For descriptions of the assumptions under each variant see table 3-1.

b. Based on adjusted family income.

carried over from the tax file for the particular years the MERGE files were prepared. The portion of the corporation income tax borne by stockholders was distributed among families on the basis of dividend income; the portion borne by property incomes in general was distributed on the basis of property incomes after tax; and the portion shifted to consumers was distributed on the basis of total money consumption. Payroll taxes were allocated on the basis of the employment incomes reported in the MERGE file, or to the extent that the payroll taxes were shifted to consumers, on the basis of total money consumption. For other taxes, the information reported for persons who had itemized deductions on their federal income tax returns was used when it was available, and the remainder was estimated on the basis of other information in the file.

Since state-local retail sales taxes, gasoline excises, income taxes, and property taxes are allowed as itemized deductions in computing federal individual income tax liability, it was necessary to estimate these taxes only for families who did not itemize deductions or did not file tax returns. The same general allocation procedure was used for each consumption tax. Total collections were first divided between the tax estimated to have been collected from business firms and the tax paid directly by households. The taxes paid by business were assumed to be shifted forward and were distributed among families in proportion to their total money consumption. The taxes paid directly by households were distributed among families that did not itemize on

JOSEPH A. PECHMAN

WHO
PAID THE
TAXES,
1966-85

STUDIES OF GOVERNMENT FINANCE
THE BROOKINGS INSTITUTION

the basis of their estimated consumption of the taxed items in the case of the specific excise taxes and on the basis of total money consumption in the case of the general sales taxes.

Income taxes were allocated by assuming that the percentage of families paying state income taxes that did not itemize was the same as the percentage of the population in income tax states. The families were selected randomly, and the tax amounts were allocated on the basis of the reported taxes of itemizing families of similar size, composition, and income.

All real estate property taxes reported as itemized deductions were assumed to be levied on owner-occupied dwellings. The amount not included in the itemized deductions was distributed among families that did not itemize deductions, or did not file returns, on the basis of the value of homes or rental payments. As was also the case with respect to the corporation income tax and the employment tax, property taxes were distributed differently under the various incidence assumptions.

CHAPTER FOUR

Distribution of Tax Burdens by Income Class

THE MAJOR RESULTS of the calculations based on the eight sets of incidence assumptions described in chapter 3 are presented in this and the following chapter. This chapter is concerned with the distribution of tax burdens in a recent year, 1980. Chapter 5 analyzes the changes in relative tax burdens from 1966 to 1985.

Distribution of Income

The distribution of adjusted family income—the basic concept used in this study to classify family units by size of income—differs from other income distributions for two reasons: first, the incomes of the sample units in the files used in this study were adjusted upward, so that when properly weighted they add to the national income aggregates; second, adjusted family income is a more comprehensive income concept than that used in other studies. To illustrate the magnitudes involved, 1980 incomes for the population as a whole on the basis of four different income concepts are compared in table 4-1.

Money income, which is the money received by members of household units as wage or salary workers, entrepreneurs, or owners of capital, plus government transfer payments, averaged $19,891 in the Consumer Population Survey (CPS) for 1980. When corrected to the national income aggregates, *average money income* increases to $23,609. The inclusion of wage supplements, accrued capital gains, imputed rent, and other adjustments to arrive at family income—the comprehensive income concept, which is derived from the national income computed at factor costs—increases average income to $31,195. Finally, the addition of indirect business taxes to obtain *adjusted family income*—the concept that corresponds to the national income

Table 4-1. *Comparison of Average Income for Family Units under Four Different Concepts, Selected Years, 1966–85*

Dollars

Income concept[a]	1966	1970	1975	1980	1985
Money income					
Unadjusted	7,542	9,609	13,185	19,891	n.a.
Adjusted	8,805	11,574	17,234	23,609	30,382
Family income, as derived from national income					
accounts	10,801	13,023	20,175	31,195	39,129
Adjusted family income	11,811	14,270	21,896	33,585	41,901

Sources: Unadjusted figures are based on data originally reported in the Survey of Economic Opportunity (1967) and Current Population Surveys (1971, 1976, and 1981). Adjusted figures are from the MERGE files and are computed under the national income incidence assumptions (variant 2a). Data for 1985 are projected.

n.a. Not available.

a. Money income is the sum of wages and salaries, interest, dividends, rents and royalties, farm and nonfarm proprietorship income, and transfer payments. For the definition of family income and adjusted family income see chapter 2.

computed at market prices—raises the average to $33,585. Adjusted family income is 69 percent more than the money income originally reported in the CPS. Similar increases in average income occur in the other years covered by this study, as the income concept is made more comprehensive (see table 4-1).

The adjustments for underreporting and nonreporting and broadening of the income concept have a significant effect on the distribution of income. As shown in table 4-2, the poorest one-fifth of the families had incomes of less than $6,610 and received 3.9 percent of total money income; the highest fifth of the families had incomes of $30,100 and over and received 44.3 percent of all income. After all the adjustments were made, the poorest fifth of the families had adjusted family income below $11,850 and received about the same share of total income, while the highest fifth moved up to $44,900 and over and received 48.7 percent of the total.[1]

The upward shift in the income distribution is most pronounced at the top. Based on data collected in the original 1980 survey, the top 5 percent included families with incomes of $49,480 and over, and they received 15.5 percent of total money income. After adjustment, the top 5 percent included families with incomes of $80,000 or more, and this group received 23.5 percent of total adjusted family income. The share of total income received by the top 1 percent of all families increased from 3.7 percent before adjustment to 11.0 percent after adjustment. This change in the income distribution results mainly from the addition of high-income family units that were omitted from

1. For this comparison, adjusted family income is computed under the national income account incidence assumptions (variant 2a).

Table 4-2. *Shares of Money Income and of Adjusted Family Income Received, by Population Quintile, 1980*

	Money income, unadjusted		Adjusted family income[a]	
Population quintile	Income range (dollars)	Percent of income received	Income range (dollars)	Percent of income received
Lowest fifth	Under 6,610	3.9	Below 11,850	4.1
Second fifth	6,610–12,660	9.8	11,850–21,350	9.8
Middle fifth	12,660–20,030	16.7	21,350–31,200	15.4
Fourth fifth	20,030–30,100	25.3	31,200–44,900	22.0
Highest fifth	30,100 and over	44.3	44,900 and over	48.7
Top 5 percent	49,480 and over	15.5	80,000 and over	23.5
Top 1 percent	67,000 and over	3.7	175,000 and over	11.0

Sources: 1981 Consumer Population Survey and 1980 Brookings MERGE file.
a. Calculated under the national income assumptions (variant 2a). For an explanation of the effect of the incidence variants on the definition of income see chapter 3.

the original CPS population and the inclusion of capital gains in adjusted family income.

The relation between the original money income distribution and the distribution of adjusted family income is shown graphically in figure 4-1, in which each distribution is represented by a Lorenz curve.[2] Clearly there is a greater concentration of income when families are arrayed by size of adjusted family income rather than by size of money income. The degree of inequality, as measured by the Gini coefficients, is greater for the distribution of adjusted family income.[3] The Gini coefficients are 0.409 and 0.445 for the 1980 Lorenz curves shown in figure 4-1.

Distribution of Tax Burdens

The distribution of tax burdens is usually presented by absolute income level, a classification that tends to exaggerate the significance of the data in some parts of the income distribution and to diminish it in other parts. The

2. See chapter 1, note 9, for an explanation of the Lorenz curve.
3. The Gini coefficient is a measure of the equality or inequality in a distribution. It is the mean of all possible differences among the observations in a distribution, regardless of signs, divided by twice the mean of the distribution. It also equals the ratio of the area between the Lorenz curve and the 45-degree line (the line of equal distribution) to the entire area below the 45-degree curve. Its value varies from zero (indicating perfect equality) to 1.0 (indicating perfect inequality). See Horst Mendershausen, *Changes in Income Distribution During the Great Depression* (National Bureau of Economic Research, 1946), pp. 162–67.

Figure 4-1. *Lorenz Curves of the Distribution of Money Income and Adjusted Family Income, 1980*

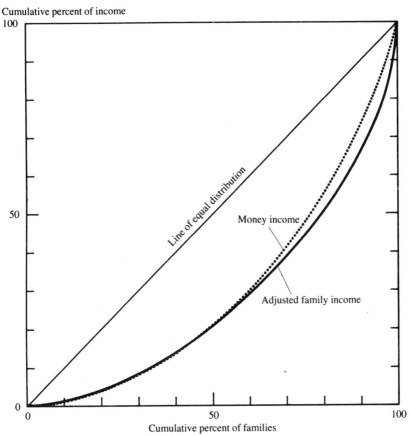

Source: Consumer Population Survey and Brookings MERGE file.

MERGE file permits the tax burden to be calculated by percentile groups as well as by absolute income levels, and thus tax burdens can be compared for groups representing the same number (or percentage) of family units in different parts of the income scale.

Tax Burdens by Absolute Income Level

Effective rates of federal, state, and local taxes in 1980 for families at different absolute income levels under the eight incidence variants are shown

Table 4-3. *Effective Rates of Federal, State, and Local Taxes under Various Incidence Assumptions, by Adjusted Family Income Class, 1980*

Percent unless otherwise specified

Adjusted family income (thousands of dollars)	Variant 1			Variant 2		Variant 3		
	a	b	c	a	b	a	b	c
0-5	33.0	32.9	32.5	38.7	47.1	43.9	57.7	35.7
5-10	20.4	20.4	20.3	22.0	23.0	24.3	26.7	21.4
10-15	21.0	21.0	20.5	21.4	22.0	23.0	24.9	21.2
15-20	21.8	21.8	21.5	21.9	22.3	23.2	25.0	21.9
20-25	23.1	23.0	22.7	23.0	23.1	24.2	25.6	23.1
25-30	23.8	23.7	23.2	23.3	23.5	24.7	25.9	23.6
30-50	25.1	25.0	24.5	24.6	24.5	25.7	26.6	24.9
50-100	27.1	27.0	26.5	26.1	25.7	26.7	26.9	26.6
100-500	27.1	27.1	27.3	26.3	26.1	24.6	24.1	26.6
500-1,000	25.0	25.1	27.0	26.9	26.6	22.3	19.8	25.9
1,000 and over	27.1	27.3	31.0	32.0	31.7	25.2	20.7	29.5
All classes[a]	25.6	25.5	25.2	25.2	25.2	25.6	26.3	25.4

Source: 1980 Brookings MERGE file. For an explanation of the incidence variants see table 3-1.
a. Includes negative incomes not shown separately.

in table 4-3. As can be seen from this table, effective tax rates are either mildly progressive or slightly regressive. Variant 1c, which distributes half the corporation income tax to stockholders and half to all property-income recipients, is the most progressive set of assumptions. Under this variant the effective tax rate is 20.3 percent for those with incomes between $5,000 and $10,000 and 31.0 percent for those with incomes of $1 million and over.[4] Variant 3b, which distributes half of the corporation income tax to property income and the other half to consumption, is regressive in the lowest part of the income scale, roughly proportional for income between $5,000 and $100,000, and regressive thereafter. Under this variant the average effective tax rate for those with incomes between $5,000 and $10,000 is 26.7 percent— 6.4 percentage points higher than under 1c; the average tax rate for families with incomes of $1 million and over is 20.7 percent—10.3 percent lower than under 1c.[5]

4. Effective rates decline sharply for all the incidence variants from the $0-$5,000 class to the $5,000-$10,000 class because numerous family units are in the lowest class only temporarily. For a discussion of the effect of this phenomenon on relative tax burdens, see the section below, "Effect of the Accounting Period on Relative Tax Burdens."
5. The reader should remember that, because adjusted family income depends upon the incidence assumptions, the families in each income class may not be the same under different

An example of the effect of different incidence assumptions can be seen by comparing the effective rates under variants 3a and 3b. The assumptions for these two variants are similar (see table 3-1), differing only with respect to the corporation income tax and payroll tax on employers. Variant 3a distributes half of the corporation income tax to dividend recipients and the other half to workers and consumers, whereas 3b distributes half of the corporation tax to property income recipients and the other half to consumers. In addition, variant 3a distributes the entire employer tax to workers on the basis of their compensation, while 3b distributes one-half of the employer tax to consumption and the other half to workers. Because families with low annual income consume a very large proportion of their incomes (in many cases, more than their incomes) and dividends are more heavily concentrated in the top classes than property income in general, low-income families are allocated a larger share of the two taxes under variant 3b than is the case under 3a. As a result, the effective tax rate is 2.4 percentage points higher in the $5,000–$10,000 class and 4.5 percentage points lower in the $1 million and over class under 3b.

Tax Burdens by Decile

The 1980 effective tax rates under the eight different incidence variants are shown in table 4-4 for families classified by population decile ranked by adjusted family income. Effective tax rates are still mildly progressive or slightly regressive, but the differences between the bottom and the top ends of the distribution are narrowed. For example, under variant 1c—the most progressive set of assumptions—the average effective rate rises from 20.6 percent in the bottom decile to 27.3 percent in the top decile and 27.5 percent in the top percentile. Under variant 3b—the least progressive set of assumptions—the average effective rate declines from 28.9 percent in the first decile to 24.6 percent in the third decile, rises to 27.2 percent in the ninth decile, and declines again to 24.9 percent in the tenth decile and 21.7 percent in the top percentile.

The effective rates for all the variants are close to one another through practically the entire distribution. The maximum difference between effective rates among all the variants is only 3.3 percentage points in the fourth decile

---

variants. This avoids the distortion in effective rates of tax that would result from misclassification. The same kind of distortion occurs whenever other definitions of income are used to classify families. For example, effective tax rates that are calculated on the basis of money income as defined by the U.S. Bureau of the Census (which is considerably smaller than adjusted family income) exaggerate the tax burdens in the higher income classes.

Table 4-4. *Effective Rates of Federal, State, and Local Taxes under Various Incidence Assumptions, by Population Decile, 1980*

Percent

Population decile	Variant 1			Variant 2		Variant 3		
	a	b	c	a	b	a	b	c
First[a]	20.6	20.7	20.6	22.9	24.9	25.1	28.9	22.2
Second	20.7	20.6	20.4	21.7	22.3	23.6	25.7	21.2
Third	21.1	21.0	20.6	21.3	21.8	22.9	24.6	21.2
Fourth	22.3	22.2	21.9	22.3	22.7	23.7	25.2	22.3
Fifth	23.4	23.3	22.8	23.1	23.2	24.5	25.8	23.3
Sixth	23.8	23.7	23.3	23.4	23.6	24.7	25.9	23.7
Seventh	24.2	24.1	23.6	23.8	23.9	25.1	26.0	24.0
Eighth	25.5	25.5	25.0	25.0	24.9	26.1	27.1	25.3
Ninth	26.4	26.3	25.7	25.6	25.4	26.5	27.2	26.0
Tenth	27.1	27.1	27.3	26.6	26.3	25.4	24.9	26.8
Top 5 percent	27.0	27.0	27.5	26.8	26.5	24.8	24.0	26.8
Top 1 percent	26.2	26.2	27.5	26.8	26.7	23.3	21.7	26.4
All deciles[b]	25.6	25.5	25.3	25.2	25.2	25.6	26.3	25.4

Source: 1980 Brookings MERGE file. For an explanation of the incidence variants see table 3-1.
a. Includes only the sixth to the tenth percentiles.
b. Includes negative incomes.

and 2.4 percentage points in the seventh decile. The differences are large only in the bottom decile, where the effective rate is 20.6 percent under variant 1c and 28.9 percent under 3b, a difference of 8.3 percentage points.

To aid the reader in interpreting table 4-4, the adjusted family incomes corresponding to the lower and upper levels of selected percentiles are given for 1980 in table 4-5. The second decile begins at income of about $7,300, the top decile, at about $60,000.[6] As table 4-4 indicates, there are significant differences in tax burdens in the bottom and top deciles under the various incidence variants.

Effect of the Accounting Period on Relative Tax Burdens

It will be noted that effective rates decline at the low end of the income scale in all variants when the population is classified by absolute income level (see table 4-3). This occurs at least in part because tax burdens com-

6. Even though families may be classified in different percentiles under the incidence variants, the reclassification does not significantly alter the absolute income limits for any particular decile of the income distribution. For example, the lowest adjusted family income for families in the top decile ranges only from $59,400 under variant 2a to $60,000 under 3b.

Table 4-5. *Adjusted Family Income under Various Incidence Assumptions, by Lower Limits of Population Deciles, 1980*

Dollars

Population decile	Variant 1			Variant 2		Variant 3		
	a	b	c	a	b	a	b	c
First[a]	0	0	0	0	0	0	0	0
Second	7,300	7,300	7,300	7,350	7,275	7,500	7,400	7,350
Third	11,800	11,800	11,750	11,850	11,750	12,050	12,000	11,825
Fourth	16,600	16,600	16,533	16,650	16,550	16,900	16,850	16,650
Fifth	21,300	21,300	21,200	21,350	21,275	21,680	21,655	21,350
Sixth	26,300	26,250	26,100	26,150	26,100	26,600	26,650	26,200
Seventh	31,325	31,250	31,100	31,200	31,100	31,650	31,750	31,250
Eighth	37,200	37,100	36,850	37,000	36,950	37,500	37,650	37,100
Ninth	45,200	45,200	44,850	44,900	44,900	45,500	45,700	45,100
Tenth	60,500	60,500	60,000	59,800	60,000	60,300	60,900	60,200
Top 5 percent	80,800	80,500	80,000	80,000	80,000	80,000	80,500	80,000
Top 1 percent	175,000	175,000	175,000	175,000	175,000	175,000	175,000	175,000

Source: 1980 Brookings MERGE file. For an explanation of the incidence variants see table 3-1.

a. The lower limit of the first decile is negative.

puted on the basis of annual income are not representative of the burdens over longer periods at this end of the income distribution. It is unfortunate that the extent of the distortion cannot be measured with the available data. Nevertheless, the factors affecting relative tax burdens when they are measured on an annual basis are understood, and the direction of some, though not all, of these influences can be evaluated in qualitative terms.

A family unit will not ordinarily make its economic decisions on the basis of income in a single year. In particular, consumption and housing decisions—and the taxes paid in connection with such decisions—will depend on the economic status of the household over a longer time period.[7] As a consequence, the effective rates of tax based on income for a single year may not be representative of the tax burdens of families with unusually low (or high) incomes.

Income in a single year may not reflect the taxpayer's longer-run economic status for a number of reasons. First, earnings may be unusually low during a particular year as a result of unemployment, illness, or other factors leading to the interruption of work. Second, adjusted family income is frequently much

7. The economic literature on this subject is large. See Robert Ferber, "Consumer Economics, A Survey," *Journal of Economic Literature,* vol. 11 (December 1973); and Angus Deaton and John Muellbauer, *Economics and Consumer Behavior* (Cambridge University Press, 1980), chap. 12.

lower than the receipts available to families of retired workers. For example, receipts from pension plans and annuities are to a large extent conversions into cash of assets accumulated from income in earlier years. The retired worker's family is likely to make its consumption decisions on the basis of its retirement benefits, even though only a small fraction of the benefits is current income as defined in this study. Third, income from many pursuits fluctuate over a period of years as a result of cyclical or other influences. There is evidence in the MERGE files that many family units suffer business losses that temporarily reduce the amount of their total income and frequently result in negative net incomes.

Taxes paid in a single year do not depend entirely on the income actually earned in that year. In many cases a family continues to consume at a level commensurate with its longer-run income and, especially in the case of families receiving retirement income, on the basis of accumulated wealth as well as income. The taxes that are affected by these factors are consumption and property taxes. For the family units involved, the ratio of these taxes to income is much higher on the basis of annual income than it is on the basis of income over a longer time. The differences are largest in the lower income classes, where retired persons as well as family units with temporarily low incomes are concentrated.[8]

Some economists believe that consumption and housing expenditures, which tend to decline with income when measured on an annual basis, may be proportional to income when measured over a period of several years.[9] If this were the case, taxes on consumption and housing would be proportional rather than regressive. Even if regressivity were not entirely eliminated, it seems clear that it would be much less pronounced over the longer run.[10]

The regressivity of total tax burdens found in the lower income levels under all the incidence variants results primarily from the regressivity of the sales and excise taxes and of the property taxes. Whether the regressivity of

8. Annual incomes also vary substantially at the top income levels; but at these levels the effect of income variability on the effective rates of consumption and property taxes is likely to be small because the ratio of consumption and housing expenditures to income is small.

9. For consumption in general see Milton Friedman, *A Theory of the Consumption Function* (Princeton University Press for the National Bureau of Economic Research, 1957); and Edgar K. Browning and William R. Johnson, *The Distribution of the Tax Burden* (American Enterprise Institute, 1979), pp. 24–27. For housing expenditures see Henry J. Aaron, *Shelter and Subsidies: Who Benefits from Federal Housing Policies?* (Brookings, 1972), pp. 212–13.

10. Multiyear data on consumption and housing outlays are not available for the very high income classes in the distributions prepared on the basis of the MERGE files for this study. It is doubtful that the alleged proportionality of consumption and housing outlays to income over a period of years extends into the top income classes.

these taxes with respect to income would remain for accounting periods longer than one year is not known. It seems clear, however, that the regressivity shown at the lowest income levels on the basis of annual figures would be moderated, if not completely eliminated, over the longer period.[11]

Effect of Taxes and Transfers on Income Distribution

Since the national tax structure appears to be proportional for a large segment of the population, it cannot have a significant effect on the distribution of income. When the before-tax and after-tax income distributions are expressed as Lorenz curves, the two curves are virtually indistinguishable. The cumulative percentages of 1980 incomes before and after taxes are shown, by decile, for variants 1c and 3b in table 4-6. Although these variants depict the extremes, the after-tax percentages are clearly very close to the before-tax percentages. The effects of taxes under the other incidence variants on the cumulative percentages of income are also small.[12]

By contrast, the effect of transfer payments on the distribution of income is pronounced. Transfers add considerably to the incomes of the lowest income classes, but less and less as incomes rise. A comparison of the effect of taxes and transfers is given in table 4-7, which ranks family units by the incomes received from the market economy (that is, adjusted family income *before* taxes and transfers) of incidence variants 1c and 3b, by decile. Since taxes are only mildly progressive under variant 1c, they reduce incomes only moderately more in the higher than in the lower deciles. On the other hand, transfers almost double market incomes in the lowest decile and increase them by only 3 percent in the top decile.

On balance, under variant 1c the family units in the lowest three deciles of market incomes receive more transfers than they pay in taxes; those in the

11. This conclusion has been confirmed on the basis of data for Canada by James Davies, France St-Hilaire, and John Whalley, "Some Calculations of Lifetime Tax Incidence," *American Economic Review,* vol. 74 (September 1984, *Papers and Proceedings, 1983*), pp. 633–49. To compensate for the overstatement of tax burdens at the lower end of the income distribution in annual data, the figures in the first decile of all the distributions presented in this volume are based on data for the sixth to the tenth decile.

12. The differences in the after-tax distributions under the different variants were more pronounced in 1966 than in 1980. See Joseph A. Pechman and Benjamin A. Okner, *Who Bears the Tax Burden?* (Brookings, 1974), pp. 55–57. However, as a result of the decline in the progressivity of the tax system between 1966 and 1980, the after-taxation distributions are quite close under all the variants in 1980.

Table 4-6. *Cumulative Distributions of Adjusted Family Income*
before and after Federal, State, and Local Taxes under Variants 1c and 3b,
by Population Decile, 1980[a]

Cumulative percentages of adjusted family income

Population decile	Variant 1c		Variant 3b	
	Before tax	*After tax*	*Before tax*	*After tax*
First	1.3	1.4	1.3	1.3
Second	4.1	4.3	4.1	4.1
Third	8.3	8.7	8.3	8.4
Fourth	13.8	14.4	13.9	14.0
Fifth	20.8	21.5	21.0	21.0
Sixth	29.2	30.0	29.5	29.4
Seventh	39.1	40.1	39.6	39.3
Eighth	51.1	52.0	51.6	51.2
Ninth	66.2	66.9	66.9	66.1
Tenth	100.0	100.0	100.0	100.0

Source: 1980 Brookings MERGE file. For an explanation of the incidence variants see table 3-1.

a. Variant 1c is the most progressive and 3b the least progressive set of incidence assumptions examined in this study. The cumulative percentages are based on distributions of family units ranked by their before-tax incomes and then reranked by their after-tax incomes.

fourth decile receive about the same amount of transfers as they pay in taxes; and those in the six highest deciles pay more in taxes than they receive in transfers. The picture is similar under variant 3b, except that taxes are roughly proportional to market incomes rather than slightly progressive throughout the scale of incomes. Thus the tax-transfer system is highly progressive under all tax incidence variants, but the progression is almost entirely the result of the transfer system (see figure 4-2). For the distributions as a whole, incomes after taxes and transfers are distributed 10 percent more equally than market incomes under 1c and 7 percent more equally under 3b (table 4-8).[13]

Tax Burdens by Type of Tax

The tax burdens presented thus far are the weighted averages of many different taxes. Some are progressive, others are regressive, and still others are progressive in some ranges of income and regressive elsewhere. This

13. The Gini coefficients in table 4-7 are based on the distribution of family units ranked by before-tax incomes and then by incomes for families ranked by after-tax incomes rather than on a comparison of the after-tax incomes of families ranked by before-tax incomes. Only the first comparison provides a basis for making a judgment about the distributional effects of the incidence assumptions.

Table 4-7. *Transfers and Taxes as a Percent of Adjusted Family Income Less Transfers under Variants 1c and 3b, by Population Decile, 1980*[a]

Population decile	Variant 1c			Variant 3b		
	Taxes	Transfers	Taxes less transfers	Taxes	Transfers	Taxes less transfers
First[b]	32.8	98.3	−65.5	50.8	101.3	−50.5
Second	22.6	58.3	−35.7	28.3	54.7	−26.4
Third	23.8	34.7	−10.9	28.3	34.8	−6.5
Fourth .	25.1	23.7	1.4	28.4	23.7	4.7
Fifth	25.9	15.3	10.6	28.9	15.6	13.3
Sixth	26.1	10.9	15.2	28.6	10.5	18.1
Seventh	26.4	7.6	18.8	28.9	7.8	21.1
Eighth	27.4	5.7	21.7	29.8	5.5	24.3
Ninth	28.3	4.3	24.0	29.9	4.4	25.5
Tenth	28.6	2.6	26.0	26.3	2.6	23.7
Top 5 percent	28.5	2.1	26.4	25.0	2.1	22.9
Top 1 percent	27.9	1.1	26.8	22.0	1.1	20.9
All classes[c]	27.5	10.0	17.5	28.5	9.9	18.6

Source: 1980 Brookings MERGE file. For an explanation of the incidence variants see table 3-1. Figures are rounded.
a. Variant 1c is the most progressive and 3b the least progressive set of incidence assumptions examined in this study.
b. Includes only sixth to tenth percentiles.
c. Includes negative income not shown separately.

section examines the contribution of the major taxes in the tax system to tax burdens at different income levels and by deciles under variants 1c and 3b. Among the eight sets of incidence assumptions examined in this study, variant 1c produces the most progressive distribution of tax burdens and variant 3b produces a regressive distribution. Hence the distributions of tax burdens under these variants represent the extremes resulting from different incidence assumptions.

The individual income tax is distributed in the same way under both sets of incidence assumptions. Revenue from this source accounts for about two-fifths of all 1980 taxes, and this obviously has an important influence on the distribution of tax burdens. The individual income tax is progressive over virtually the entire income scale, but it becomes slightly regressive at the very top. This pattern reflects the fact that in the highest income classes a rising portion of total income as defined in this study is not subject to income tax at either the federal or the state level.[14] The individual income tax imposes the

14. For a discussion of the items not subject to the federal income tax, see Joseph A. Pechman and John Karl Scholz, "Comprehensive Income Taxation and Rate Reduction," *Tax Notes* (October 11, 1982), pp. 83–93 (Brookings Reprint 390).

Figure 4-2. *Federal, State, and Local Transfers and Taxes as a Percent of Market Income, by Population Percentile, 1980*[a]

Percent of market incomes

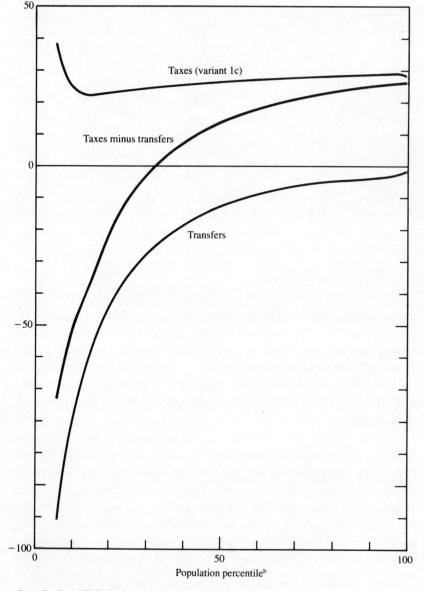

Source: Brookings MERGE file. For an explanation of the incidence variants see table 3-1.
a. Market income equals adjusted family income minus transfers.
b. Arrayed by size of market incomes.

Table 4-8. *Gini Coefficients for the Distribution of Income before and after Transfers and Taxes under Variants 1c and 3b, 1980*[a]

Incidence variant	Before transfers and before taxes[b]	After transfers and before taxes[c]	After transfers and after taxes[d]
1c	0.483	0.445	0.435
3b	0.477	0.440	0.444

Source: 1980 Brookings MERGE file. For an explanation of the incidence variants see table 3-1.

a. The Gini coefficient is the ratio of the area between a Lorenz curve and the 45-degree line (the line of equal distribution) to the entire area below the 45-degree line. These coefficients are based on distributions of families ranked by their before-tax and before-transfer incomes, then reranked by their after-transfer and before-tax incomes, and finally reranked by their after-transfer and after-tax incomes.

b. Adjusted family income less transfers.

c. Adjusted family income.

d. Adjusted family income less taxes.

heaviest burden on incomes between $100,000 and $500,000—13.9 percent of adjusted family income under variant 1c and 14.4 percent under 3b (see table 4-9).

The difference in the effective rates of individual income tax at the same income level result entirely from the different definitions of income used in the two sets of assumptions. Under variant 1c, the corporation income tax and the property tax on improvements are included in adjusted family incomes of stockholders and property-income recipients; under variant 3b, half the corporation income tax and the entire property tax on improvements are regarded as indirect taxes and are distributed among all family units in calculating adjusted family income.[15] As a consequence, stockholders and property-income recipients have much higher adjusted family incomes under variant 1c than under 3b, and the burden of the individual income tax relative to incomes at the top of the income scale (where dividends and other property incomes are large) is reduced.

Sales and excise taxes are clearly regressive throughout the entire income scale. In 1980 they began at almost 18 percent of income at the bottom and declined to less than 1 percent at the top, reflecting the fact that the proportion of family income spent on goods and services subject to tax falls as income rises. The small differences in the effective rates of these taxes at particular income levels also reflect the different definitions of income used in the two variants.

Payroll taxes, which are levied at a flat rate up to a maximum amount of annual taxable earnings, are also regressive throughout the income scale. Since employer and employee taxes are both assumed to be borne by workers in variant 1c, 1980 payroll taxes declined from 9.4 percent of income at the

15. See the discussion of the relation between the tax concept and the definition of income in chapter 3.

Table 4-9. *Effective Rates of Federal, State, and Local Taxes under Variants 1c and 3b, by Adjusted Family Income Class, 1980*[a]

Percent unless otherwise specified

Adjusted family income (thousands of dollars)	Individual income taxes	Corporation income tax	Property tax	Sales and excise taxes	Payroll taxes	Personal property and motor vehicle taxes	Total taxes
			Variant 1c				
0–5	3.2	0.8	1.0	17.9	9.4	0.3	32.5
5–10	2.7	0.5	0.6	7.7	8.7	0.1	20.3
10–15	4.9	0.7	0.9	6.2	7.7	0.1	20.5
15–20	6.5	0.8	0.9	5.6	7.6	0.2	21.5
20–25	7.8	0.8	1.0	5.2	7.6	0.2	22.7
25–30	8.6	0.9	1.2	4.9	7.3	0.3	23.2
30–50	10.5	1.2	1.4	4.5	6.7	0.3	24.5
50–100	13.1	2.3	2.2	3.3	5.4	0.2	26.5
100–500	13.9	5.7	3.9	1.6	2.1	0.1	27.3
500–1,000	10.8	9.7	5.2	0.7	0.5	0.1	27.1
1,000 and over	11.3	13.1	5.8	0.6	0.2	0.0	31.0
All classes[b]	10.8	2.5	2.0	4.0	5.8	0.2	25.3
			Variant 3b				
0–5	3.5	9.7	7.9	19.5	16.7	0.3	57.7
5–10	2.6	3.6	3.0	7.6	9.8	0.1	26.7
10–15	4.7	3.1	2.4	6.1	8.5	0.1	24.9
15–20	6.2	2.9	2.1	5.5	8.1	0.2	25.0
20–25	7.5	2.7	2.1	5.2	7.9	0.2	25.6
25–30	8.4	2.7	2.1	4.8	7.6	0.2	25.9
30–50	10.1	2.7	2.2	4.4	7.0	0.3	26.6
50–100	12.8	2.9	2.3	3.3	5.5	0.2	26.9
100–500	14.4	3.4	2.2	1.6	2.4	0.1	24.1
500–1,000	11.9	4.1	2.2	0.8	0.8	0.1	19.8
1,000 and over	12.6	4.6	2.3	0.6	0.4	0.0	20.7
All classes[b]	10.7	3.0	2.3	4.0	6.1	0.2	26.3

Source: 1980 Brookings MERGE file. For an explanation of the incidence variants see table 3-1.
a. Variant 1c is the most progressive and 3b the least progressive set of incidence assumptions examined in this study.
b. Includes negative incomes not shown separately.

bottom of the income scale to 0.2 percent at the top. In variant 3b half of the employer payroll tax is assumed to be shifted to the consumer through higher prices; as a result the effective payroll tax rate at the bottom end of the distribution increased sharply from 9.4 percent to 16.7 percent.[16]

16. Since a major share of the payroll taxes is allocated to the retirement and disability funds, some economists argue that benefits should be netted out against the taxes that are earmarked to pay them. This is done for all transfer payments in table 4-8.

Personal property taxes and motor vehicle license taxes were slightly progressive up to incomes of about $50,000 and regressive thereafter. The effect of these taxes on relative tax burdens was small—they amount to no more than 0.3 percent of income throughout the income scale.

The crucial factors in determining the degree of progressivity in the tax system as a whole are the assumptions made with respect to the incidence of the corporation income tax and the property tax. If it is assumed that these are taxes on corporate stockholders and owners of property (variant 1c), they are highly progressive. On this assumption, the 1980 corporation income tax rose from less than 1 percent of income at the bottom of the income scale to over 13 percent at the top; the property tax rose from 1 percent to nearly 6 percent.[17] Assuming that half of the corporation income tax is a tax on consumption and that the property taxes on improvements are taxes on shelter and consumption (variant 3b), the progressivity of these taxes virtually disappears. Since the ratio of total consumption and housing expenditures to annual income falls as incomes rise, the burden of the corporation and property taxes under variant 3b is U-shaped, but the rise in the effective rates of these two taxes in the top decile is small. Together these two taxes amounted to 6.9 percent of income for families with incomes above $1 million under variant 3b, as compared with a total of 18.9 percent under 1c.

When the effective rates of the various taxes are examined by decile (see table 4-10), the picture changes only in details. Since all families with incomes of about $60,000 and over are grouped in the top income decile, differences in the effective tax rates at the top of the income scale are muted. For example, when families are grouped by decile, as in table 4-10, the individual income tax appears progressive throughout the income scale, even though it is slightly regressive at the very highest income level. Similarly, while the general pattern of rates found for other taxes does not change when families are classified by deciles, extreme values at both ends of the income scale are brought down. Thus the 1980 corporation tax rate in the top decile under variant 1c was only 5.0 percent (table 4-10) compared with 13.1 percent for the highest income class ($1 million and over) in table 4-9. The effective payroll tax rate under this variant moves in the opposite direction in the two tables: in table 4-9 the average effective payroll rate in the highest income class is 0.2 percent; in table 4-10, the rate in the highest decile is 3.2 percent.

17. The decline in the effective rates of these taxes at the $5,000 income level reflects the fact that low-income, aged persons receive relatively large proportions of their income from property in the form of interest and dividends and, in the case of home owners, imputed rent.

Table 4-10. *Effective Rates of Federal, State, and Local Taxes under Variants 1c and 3b, by Population Decile, 1980*[a]

Percent

Population decile	Individual income taxes	Corporation income tax	Property tax	Sales and excise taxes	Payroll taxes	Personal property and motor vehicle taxes	Total taxes
			Variant 1c				
First[b]	2.1	0.6	0.7	8.4	8.8	0.1	20.6
Second	3.8	0.5	0.7	7.0	8.3	0.1	20.4
Third	5.3	0.7	0.9	5.9	7.6	0.1	20.6
Fourth	6.8	0.8	0.9	5.5	7.5	0.2	21.9
Fifth	8.0	0.9	1.0	5.1	7.5	0.2	22.8
Sixth	8.8	0.9	1.2	4.9	7.2	0.3	23.3
Seventh	9.5	1.1	1.2	4.6	6.8	0.3	23.6
Eighth	11.0	1.2	1.3	4.5	6.7	0.3	25.0
Ninth	12.1	1.6	1.7	3.9	6.1	0.2	25.7
Tenth	13.4	5.0	3.5	2.1	3.2	0.1	27.3
Top 5 percent	13.4	6.1	4.0	1.6	2.2	0.1	27.5
Top 1 percent	12.5	8.2	4.7	1.0	1.0	0.1	27.5
All deciles[c]	10.8	2.5	2.0	4.0	5.8	0.2	25.3
			Variant 3b				
First[b]	2.2	4.1	3.5	8.7	10.3	0.1	28.9
Second	3.6	3.3	2.6	6.8	9.2	0.1	25.7
Third	5.3	3.0	2.2	5.8	8.3	0.2	24.6
Fourth	6.7	2.8	2.1	5.4	8.0	0.2	25.2
Fifth	7.8	2.7	2.1	5.0	7.9	0.2	25.8
Sixth	8.6	2.7	2.1	4.8	7.5	0.3	25.9
Seventh	9.2	2.7	2.1	4.5	7.1	0.3	26.0
Eighth	10.7	2.7	2.2	4.3	6.9	0.3	27.1
Ninth	11.9	2.7	2.2	3.9	6.3	0.2	27.2
Tenth	13.6	3.3	2.2	2.1	3.4	0.2	24.9
Top 5 percent	13.9	3.5	2.2	1.7	2.5	0.1	24.0
Top 1 percent	13.2	3.8	2.2	1.1	1.3	0.1	21.7
All deciles[c]	10.7	3.0	2.3	4.0	6.1	0.2	26.3

Source: 1980 Brookings MERGE file. For an explanation of the incidence variants see table 3-1.

a. Variant 1c is the most progressive and 3b the least progressive set of incidence assumptions examined in this study.

b. Includes only units in the sixth to tenth percentiles.

c. Includes negative incomes not shown separately.

Burdens of Federal versus State and Local Taxes

In 1980, 94 percent of federal tax revenue was obtained from the individual income, corporation income, and payroll taxes. The states and localities relied primarily on general sales and excise taxes and the property tax. These differences in revenue sources create substantial differences in relative tax burdens at the federal and the state-local levels.

Effective tax rates for federal and state-local taxes in 1980—again shown only for variants 1c and 3b—are given in table 4-11. Federal taxes are progressive under 1c, but they are roughly proportional under 3b. Under 1c the effective tax rate for family units with incomes of $1 million and over was almost twice as high as the rate in the $5,000–$10,000 class; under 3b the effective rate was about the same in both income classes. Again, these differences reflect different assumptions as to the incidence of the corporation income tax under the two variants. Variant 3b allocates a substantial portion of this tax to low- and middle-income families. As a result, the federal tax burden is increased by 3.6 percentage points for those with incomes of $5,000 to $10,000; correspondingly, the federal tax burden at the top of the income scale is reduced by 5.8 percentage points.

Although state-local taxes are generally believed to be regressive, this conclusion holds only under a specific set of incidence assumptions. Under variant 3b, which allocates property taxes on improvements on the basis of outlays for shelter and total consumption, effective state and local tax rates are regressive throughout the income scale. On these assumptions, state-local taxes for those at the top of the income scale amounted to only about 5 percent of income in 1980.

The picture changes dramatically when property taxes on improvements are allocated on the basis of property ownership. Under variant 1c the average effective state-local tax rates in 1980 had a U-shaped pattern, which began at about 18 percent for families with incomes under $5,000, declined to about 7 percent for incomes between $10,000 and $100,000, and then rose to almost 10 percent for those with incomes of $1 million and over.

As was the case earlier, when families are arrayed by relative rather than absolute income levels, the average effective tax rates at the high end of the income scale are moderated considerably in the decile distribution. Thus in table 4-12 effective federal rates in 1980 under variant 1c rose to 19.4 percent in the top decile, compared with 21.4 percent for the highest income class ($1 million and over) in table 4-11. The state-local tax rate in the top decile

Table 4-11. *Effective Rates of Federal and of State and Local Taxes under Variants 1c and 3b, by Adjusted Family Income Class, 1980*[a]

Percent unless otherwise specified

Percent

Population decile	Variant 1c			Variant 3b		
	Federal tax	State and local taxes	Total taxes	Federal tax	State and local taxes	Total taxes
0-5	14.2	18.3	32.5	29.8	27.9	57.7
5-10	12.2	8.1	20.3	15.8	10.9	26.7
10-15	13.3	7.2	20.5	15.9	9.0	24.9
15-20	14.5	7.0	21.5	16.6	8.3	25.0
20-25	15.7	6.9	22.7	17.4	8.2	25.6
25-30	16.2	7.0	23.2	17.8	8.1	25.9
30-50	17.4	7.2	24.5	18.6	8.0	26.6
50-100	19.1	7.4	26.5	19.5	7.5	26.9
100-500	19.2	8.1	27.3	18.0	6.1	24.1
500-1,000	18.2	8.9	27.1	14.6	5.2	19.8
1,000 and over	21.4	9.7	31.0	15.6	5.1	20.7
All classes[b]	17.7	7.5	25.3	18.5	7.8	26.3

Source: 1980 Brookings MERGE file. For an explanation of incidence variants see table 3-1. Details may not add to totals because of rounding.

a. Variant 1c is the most progressive and 3b the least progressive set of incidence assumptions examined in this study.

b. Includes negative incomes not shown separately.

(shown in table 4-12) is 7.9 percent, one-sixth lower than the 9.7 percent rate shown in table 4-11 for those with incomes of $1 million and over.

The general shape of effective tax rates by income level is not changed if families are classified by relative, rather than by absolute, income level. In 1980, federal tax rates were progressive above the first decile under variants 1c and 3b, while state-local rates retained their regressive pattern under variant 3b and their U-shaped pattern under variant 1c.

Summary

The tax system in 1980 was only mildly progressive or slightly regressive, depending on the incidence assumptions. Under the most progressive set of assumptions examined in this study (variant 1c), taxes reduced income inequality by 2.5 percent; under the least progressive assumptions (3b), income inequality was increased by about 0.8 percent.

On the other hand, the transfer system is highly progressive. Transfer payments exceeded taxes in the first three deciles, while taxes exceeded transfers in the top six deciles. In the fourth decile transfers and taxes were

Table 4-12. *Effective Rates of Federal and of State and Local Taxes, Variants 1c and 3b, by Population Decile, 1980*[a]

Percent

Population decile	Variant 1c			Variant 3b		
	Federal tax	State and local taxes	Total taxes	Federal tax	State and local taxes	Total taxes
First[b]	11.7	9.0	20.6	16.3	12.6	28.9
Second	12.8	7.6	20.4	15.9	9.8	25.7
Third	13.6	7.1	20.6	16.1	8.5	24.6
Fourth	14.8	7.0	21.9	16.9	8.3	25.2
Fifth	15.9	6.9	22.8	17.6	8.1	25.8
Sixth	16.3	7.0	23.3	17.8	8.0	25.9
Seventh	16.6	7.0	23.6	18.0	8.0	26.0
Eighth	17.8	7.2	25.0	19.0	8.0	27.1
Ninth	18.4	7.3	25.7	19.3	7.9	27.2
Tenth	19.4	7.9	27.3	18.4	6.5	24.9
Top 5 percent	19.4	8.1	27.5	17.9	6.1	24.0
Top 1 percent	18.9	8.6	27.5	16.2	5.5	21.7
All deciles[c]	17.7	7.5	25.3	18.5	7.8	26.3

Source: 1980 Brookings MERGE file. For an explanation of the incidence variants see table 3-1. Figures are rounded.

a. Variant 1c is the most progressive and 3b the least progressive set of incidence assumptions examined in this study.

b. Includes only the sixth to tenth percentiles.

c. Includes negative incomes not shown separately.

roughly equal. Incomes after taxes and transfers are 7–10 percent more equally distributed than incomes before taxes and transfers, but this was the result mainly of the transfer system.

Effective tax rates are high at both the bottom and the top of the income scale. The high rates for those in the lowest income classes are probably not indicative of their tax burdens over longer periods, because in these classes there is a heavy concentration of retired persons and of individuals whose incomes are low temporarily. The very rich pay high taxes because a substantial portion of their income comes from property. If it is assumed that the corporation income and property taxes are taxes on income from capital, the tax burden of families with incomes of $1 million and over was 31 percent in 1980, almost 50 percent *higher* than the rates paid by most families. If these taxes are assumed to be shifted in whole or in part to consumers, the tax burden at the higher income level was only about 21 percent, or about 20 percent *lower* than the effective rates paid by most families.

The crucial nature of the incidence assumptions in evaluating the progressivity of a tax system is evident when effective rates of federal and state-local taxes are compared. State-local taxes are generally believed to be regressive, but this depends on the assumed incidence of the property tax. If the property tax is regarded as a tax on owners of capital, state-local tax burdens had a U-shaped pattern in 1980, with the lightest burdens on families with incomes from $10,000 to $50,000. Federal taxes were progressive throughout the income scale (except for the lowest income class) under all the incidence assumptions used in this study.

CHAPTER FIVE

Changes in the Distribution of Tax Burdens, 1966–85

CALCULATIONS of tax burdens similar to those reported in chapter 4 for 1980 were made for the years 1966, 1970, 1975, and 1985. The 1966, 1970, and 1975 calculations were prepared on the basis of the MERGE files for those years; the 1980 and 1985 calculations are based on projections of the 1975 file.[1] The 1985 tax calculations are estimates based on federal, state, and local tax legislation enacted as of January 1, 1984. Taken together, these figures provide a series of snapshots depicting tax burdens for the U.S. population over a period of almost two decades. Before analyzing the trends in the distribution of tax burdens, it will be useful to identify the more significant changes in tax policy affecting tax burdens during this period.[2]

Legislative History

It is useful to start with the Revenue Act of 1964, which set the structural features of the federal income taxes for the rest of the 1960s. The act reduced individual income tax rates by an average of 20 percent, with the bottom rate going from 20 percent to 14 percent and the top rate from 91 percent to 70 percent. An investment tax credit and liberalized depreciation allowances had been introduced in 1962 and the 1964 act reduced the general corporation tax rate from 52 to 48 percent. These changes were the first of many during the period covered by this study that greatly reduced the effective corporation tax rates.

1. For the assumptions used in the projections, see chapter 2.
2. Clearly, a brief review of tax developments over two decades can hardly do justice to the subject. The interested reader is encouraged to consult more detailed references. See, for example, Joseph A. Pechman, *Federal Tax Policy* (Brookings, 1983).

In 1965, Congress passed a major excise tax reduction bill, effective in mid-1965. This bill scaled down the Korean war excise taxes to all but a few major taxes levied for sumptuary and regulatory reasons and user charges. Many of the excise taxes are levied on a specific basis (for example, cents per gallon or per 100 cigarettes) and remained at the level enacted in 1965 until 1982. Because of the large intervening inflation, receipts from federal excise taxes did not keep pace with the growth of nominal incomes throughout the period.

The only major change made in the excise tax structure since 1965 was the introduction of special taxes to finance the Airport and Airway Trust Fund in 1970. In 1982, taxes to finance the highways and airways were raised and the cigarette tax was increased from eight cents to sixteen cents for the period from January 1, 1983, to September 30, 1985.

The Tax Reform Act of 1969 was enacted in response to public pressure for tax revision generated by a statement from outgoing Secretary of the Treasury Joseph J. Barr that 155 taxpayers with incomes above $200,000 had not paid any tax in 1967. The act relieved a large number of low-income people from paying federal income taxes by increasing the personal exemption and standard deduction, introduced a minimum tax for high-income individuals and corporations, and reduced the maximum tax rate on earnings (wages and salaries and self-employment incomes) from 70 percent to 50 percent.

During the early 1970s, federal tax bills were passed frequently, some of relatively minor significance but cumulating to significant change. The Revenue Act of 1971 introduced the Accelerated Depreciation Range (ADR) system of depreciation, continuing the trend toward more liberal depreciation allowances begun a decade earlier. The Pension Reform Act of 1974 initiated the use of Individual Retirement Accounts (IRAs) to permit the accumulation of tax-free saving for retirement purposes by those who were not covered by employer retirement plans. The Tax Reduction Act of 1975 increased the personal exemptions through the use of a tax credit, introduced an earned income credit for low-income recipients, and raised the investment tax credit from 7 percent to 10 percent.

The Tax Reform Act of 1976 lengthened the holding period for the reduced rate on capital gains from six months to a year. The Tax Reduction and Simplification Act of 1977 increased the amount of nontaxable income that could be earned by introducing the zero bracket amount at a higher level than the previous low-income allowance. The Revenue Act of 1978 converted the credit enacted two years earlier to the equivalent exemption. It also reduced the tax rate on long-term capital gains from 50 percent to 40 percent of the tax rates on ordinary income. Energy tax credits were introduced in 1980, and a windfall profits tax on oil and gas was enacted in 1980.

The major piece of legislation affecting the 1980s was the Economic Recovery Tax Act of 1981 (ERTA). This act reduced individual income tax rates by 23 percent over a period of three years, cut the top rate on unearned income from 70 percent to 50 percent, and adjusted the individual income tax rate brackets, exemptions, and zero bracket amounts for inflation beginning in 1985. It also permitted individuals not covered by private pension plans to invest in tax-free IRAs, and introduced a deduction for net interest received beginning in 1985.[3]

Depreciation allowances for tax purposes were further liberalized in 1981 by the substitution of the Accelerated Cost Recovery System (ACRS) for ADR. The Tax Equity and Fiscal Responsibility Act of 1982 (TEFRA) reduced these allowances somewhat (but they remained much more liberal than the ADR allowances), required taxpayers to reduce the basis for depreciation purposes by half the investment credit, and introduced a new, somewhat higher minimum tax for both individuals and corporations.[4]

Aside from income tax legislation, the major influence on the distribution of tax burdens has been the increase in payroll taxes. From 1966 to 1985 the social security payroll tax rate for both employers and employees increased from 4.2 percent to 7.05 percent, and the maximum taxable earnings level rose from $6,600 in 1966 to an estimated $39,000 in 1985, about twice as fast as the change in the consumer price index. Payroll taxes for the unemployment compensation system also increased during the period. The rate for this tax increased from 3.1 percent on wages up to $3,000 in 1966 to a scheduled 6.2 percent on wages up to $7,000 in 1985.

State and local governments raised their income and sales tax rates during the period, while the effective rate of property taxation declined. On balance, state and local taxes rose from 9.4 percent of the gross national product in 1966 to 12.2 percent in 1977, and then declined to 11.3 percent in 1980.

The net effect of these changes on the roles of the various taxes is summarized in table 5-1, using the aggregates based on the variant 1c assumptions.

3. The deduction, which was 15 percent of total interest reported less interest paid up to a maximum of $6,000 for married couples and $3,000 for single people, was repealed in 1984 (see note 4).

4. The Tax Reform Act of 1984 was enacted after the calculations for this study were completed. The major change in the act was repeal of the net interest deduction enacted in 1981, reduction of the holding period for capital gains from a year to six months, and an increase in the period over which depreciation for real estate is calculated. The effect of these changes on the 1985 distribution of tax burdens is small.

Table 5-1. *Ratio of Federal and of State and Local Taxes to Adjusted Family Income under Variant 1c, Selected Years, 1966-85*[a]

Percent

Year	Individual income taxes	Corporation income tax	Property tax	Sales and excise taxes	Payroll taxes	Personal property and motor vehicle taxes	Total taxes
			Total taxes				
1966	8.5	3.9	3.0	5.1	4.4	0.3	25.2
1970	9.7	2.6	3.3	5.3	4.9	0.3	26.1
1975	9.3	2.5	2.8	4.5	5.7	0.3	25.0
1980	10.8	2.5	2.0	4.0	5.8	0.2	25.2
1985	10.9	1.8	2.0	3.4	6.2	0.2	24.5
			Federal taxes				
1966	7.7	3.7	. . .	1.8	4.4	. . .	17.6
1970	8.6	2.3	. . .	1.6	4.9	. . .	17.4
1975	8.0	2.1	. . .	1.0	5.7	. . .	16.7
1980	9.2	2.1	. . .	0.7	5.8	. . .	17.7
1985	9.0	1.4	. . .	0.6	6.2	. . .	17.2
			State and local taxes				
1966	0.8	0.3	3.0	3.3	. . .	0.3	7.6
1970	1.1	0.3	3.3	3.7	. . .	0.3	8.7
1975	1.4	0.3	2.8	3.5	. . .	0.3	8.3
1980	1.6	0.3	2.0	3.3	. . .	0.2	7.5
1985	1.9	0.4	2.0	2.9	. . .	0.2	7.3

Source: Brookings MERGE files. Figures are rounded.

a. Variant 1c is the most progressive set of incidence assumptions used in this study.

Total federal, state, and local taxes varied only slightly during this period as a percentage of adjusted family income, rising from 25.2 percent in 1966 to 26.1 percent in 1970 and then declining to 24.5 percent in 1985. However, there were significant changes in the relative importance of the various tax sources. Federal, state, and local individual income taxes increased gradually from 8.5 percent of adjusted family income to 1966 to 10.9 percent in 1985. Payroll taxes rose sharply between these years, from 4.4 percent to 6.2 percent. On the other hand, the corporation income tax declined from 3.9 percent to 1.8 percent of adjusted family income, sales and excise taxes from 5.1 percent to 3.4 percent, and the property tax from 3.0 percent to 2.0 percent. Thus there was a decline in two major progressive sources (the corporation income tax and the property tax) and a rise in a major regressive source (the payroll tax), which was only partially offset by the decline in the regressive sales and excise taxes and the increase in the individual income taxes. Moreover, federal individual tax rates in the top brackets were reduced sharply in 1981. These broad trends suggest that the progressivity of the tax system declined between 1966 and 1985.

Changes in Effective Tax Rates

The data in table 5-2, which summarize the changes in the effective rates of tax by population decile for variants 1c and 3b, confirm the decline in the progressivity of the tax system from 1966 to 1985. In 1966, federal, state, and local taxes rose from 16.8 percent of adjusted family income in the lowest decile to 30.1 percent in the top decile under the most progressive assumptions (variant 1c). Between 1966 and 1985 the tax burdens increased in the two lowest deciles, remained about the same in the third and fourth deciles, rose slightly in the fifth to the ninth deciles, but declined in the highest decile. By 1985 the effective tax rate had risen to 21.9 percent in the lowest decile and declined to 25.3 percent at the top. Thus the ratio of the tax burden in the highest to that in the lowest decile fell from 1.79 to 1.16.

The least progressive set of assumptions (variant 3b) tells a similar story. Between 1966 and 1985 the tax burdens remained about the same in the third to the ninth decile, but they changed at the top and the bottom of the income distribution. In the lowest decile the effective tax rate rose from 27.5 percent in 1966 to 28.2 percent in 1985. In the highest decile the effective rate declined from 25.9 percent to 23.3 percent. The ratio of the tax burden in the highest to that in the lowest decile declined from 0.94 to 0.83.

Changes in the Burdens of Various Taxes

The major reason for the increase in the tax burden at the lower end of the income scale from 1966 to 1985 was the rise in payroll taxes. In the first decile, payroll taxes amounted to 2.6 percent of adjusted family income in 1966 under variant 1c and 9.4 percent in 1985. Individual income taxes also rose significantly—in the first decile from 1.1 percent to 4.2 percent of adjusted family income—partly as a result of the failure to adjust the personal exemptions and standard deduction for the inflation in the late 1970s and partly as a result of income growth during the entire period. These increases were partially offset by reductions in both the corporation and property taxes (from a combined total of 3.8 percent of adjusted family income in 1966 to 1.2 percent in 1985), but the increases outweighed the reductions (see the appendix).

Table 5-2. *Effective Rates of Federal, State, and Local Taxes under Variants*
1c and 3b, by Population Decile, Selected Years, 1966-85[a]

Percent

Population decile	1966	1970	1975	1980	1985
			Variant 1c		
First[b]	16.8	18.8	21.2	20.6	21.9
Second	18.9	19.5	19.9	20.4	21.3
Third	21.7	20.8	20.5	20.6	21.4
Fourth	22.6	23.2	22.0	21.9	22.5
Fifth	22.8	24.0	23.0	22.8	23.1
Sixth	22.7	24.1	23.3	23.3	23.5
Seventh	22.7	24.3	23.6	23.6	23.7
Eighth	23.1	24.6	24.4	25.0	24.6
Ninth	23.3	25.0	25.3	25.7	25.1
Tenth	30.1	30.7	27.1	27.3	25.3
All deciles[c]	25.2	26.1	25.0	25.2	24.5
			Variant 3b		
First[b]	27.5	25.8	29.6	28.9	28.2
Second	24.8	24.2	24.2	25.7	25.6
Third	26.0	24.2	23.4	24.6	24.6
Fourth	25.9	25.9	24.6	25.2	25.2
Fifth	25.8	26.4	25.3	25.8	25.3
Sixth	25.6	26.2	25.3	25.9	25.6
Seventh	25.5	26.2	25.5	26.0	25.4
Eighth	25.5	26.4	26.0	27.1	26.3
Ninth	25.1	26.1	26.3	27.2	26.1
Tenth	25.9	27.8	24.2	24.9	23.3
All deciles[c]	25.9	26.7	25.5	26.3	25.3

Source: Brookings MERGE files. Figures are rounded.
a. Variant 1c is the most progressive and 3b is the least progressive set of incidence assumptions used in this study.
b. Includes only units in the sixth to tenth percentiles.
c. Includes negative incomes not shown separately.

In the top decile the effective rate of tax fell between 1966 and 1985 mainly because of reductions in the corporation and property taxes. Under variant 1c the corporation income tax declined from 8.1 percent of adjusted family income in 1966 to 3.6 percent in 1985, and the property tax declined from 5.1 percent to 3.3 percent. Individual income, sales, and payroll taxes rose in this decile, but not enough to offset the large reductions in the corporation and property taxes.

Table 5-3. *Effective Rates of Federal Individual Income Tax and Corporation Income Tax under Variants 1c and 3b, by Population Decile, 1980 and 1985*[a]

Percent

Population decile	Individual income tax		Corporation income tax	
	1980	1985	1980	1985
	Variant 1c			
First[b]	1.1	3.1	0.5	0.4
Second	3.0	4.5	0.5	0.4
Third	4.4	5.8	0.6	0.5
Fourth	5.7	6.9	0.7	0.5
Fifth	6.7	7.6	0.7	0.5
Sixth	7.4	8.1	0.8	0.6
Seventh	8.0	8.5	1.0	0.7
Eighth	9.3	9.4	1.0	0.7
Ninth	10.3	10.0	1.4	1.0
Tenth	11.5	10.3	4.3	2.9
All deciles[c]	9.2	9.0	2.1	1.4
	Variant 3b			
First[b]	1.1	2.9	3.6	2.2
Second	2.8	4.5	2.9	1.8
Third	4.3	5.7	2.6	1.6
Fourth	5.5	6.7	2.4	1.6
Fifth	6.6	7.4	2.3	1.5
Sixth	7.2	8.0	2.3	1.5
Seventh	7.8	8.3	2.3	1.5
Eighth	9.0	9.2	2.3	1.5
Ninth	10.1	9.8	2.4	1.5
Tenth	11.7	10.5	2.9	1.8
All deciles[c]	9.1	9.0	2.6	1.7

Source: Brookings MERGE files.
a. Variant 1c is the most progressive and 3b is the least progressive set of incidence assumptions used in this study.
b. Includes only units in the sixth to tenth percentiles.
c. Includes negative incomes not shown separately.

Effect of the 1981 Federal Tax Cuts

The changes in effective rates of tax resulting from the federal tax reductions enacted in 1981 are reflected primarily in the tax burdens of the top decile. Between 1980 and 1985 effective federal individual income tax rates under variant 1c rose in the first seven deciles by an average of about 1 percentage point, remained about the same in the eighth and ninth deciles, and declined 1.2 points in the top decile (table 5-3). The higher tax burdens at the

70

lower end of the income scale is the result of increases in effective tax rates generated by inflation;[5] and these increases were enough to offset the effect of the 23 percent reduction in individual income tax rates that became effective during this period. At the top end, the federal individual income tax burden declined from 11.5 percent of adjusted family income to 10.3 percent because the rate reductions and other structural changes of the 1981 act (notably the reduction in the long-term capital gains rate and the increase in deductions for IRAs) more than offset the effect of income increases in this decile. The changes in effective federal individual income tax rates during this period are roughly the same under variant 3b because the incidence assumptions are the same under variants 1c and 3b.

Effective federal corporation income tax rates under variant 1c declined throughout the income distribution between 1980 and 1985 (table 5-3), but the decline was significant only in the top decile, where it fell from 4.3 percent to 2.9 percent of income, or by almost a third. The decline was most pronounced at the top end of the distribution because under variant 1c the corporation income tax is assumed to be borne by property income, which is heavily concentrated in the highest income classes. The decline in effective federal corporation income tax rates is more pronounced in all deciles except the top two under variant 3b than under 1c because half the corporation tax is assumed to be shifted to consumers under this set of assumptions.

Changes in the Federal and the State and Local Tax Systems

The decline in the progressivity of the tax system between 1966 and 1985 is accounted for entirely by changes in the federal tax system. The state-local tax system remained slightly U-shaped or regressive, depending on the incidence assumptions, and the effective rates in each decile did not change much.

Under variant 1c, federal taxes in 1966 rose from 7.8 percent of adjusted family income in the first decile to 21.1 percent in the top decile. By 1985, largely as a result of the decline in the corporation income tax and the rise in payroll taxes, federal taxes increased to 13.9 percent of adjusted family income in the first decile, but declined to 17.1 percent in the top decile. State

---

5. Between 1980 and 1985 the average adjusted family income under variant 1c rose 24 percent. This compares with an estimated increase in the gross national product deflator of more than 30 percent.

Table 5-4. *Effective Rates of Federal and of State and Local Taxes under Variants 1c and 3b, by Population Decile, 1966 and 1985*[a]

Percent

Population decile	Federal 1966	Federal 1985	State and local 1966	State and local 1985
	Variant 1c			
First[b]	7.8	13.9	9.1	8.0
Second	10.2	14.5	8.6	6.8
Third	13.5	15.0	8.2	6.5
Fourth	15.1	16.0	7.5	6.5
Fifth	15.9	16.7	6.9	6.4
Sixth	16.1	16.9	6.6	6.6
Seventh	16.2	17.0	6.5	6.7
Eighth	16.6	17.8	6.5	6.9
Ninth	16.7	18.0	6.6	7.1
Tenth	21.1	17.1	9.0	8.1
All deciles[c]	17.6	17.2	7.6	7.3
	Variant 3b			
First[b]	13.8	16.9	13.7	11.3
Second	13.7	16.7	11.1	8.9
Third	15.8	16.7	10.2	7.9
Fourth	16.8	17.4	9.1	7.8
Fifth	17.4	17.7	8.4	7.6
Sixth	17.4	17.9	8.2	7.7
Seventh	17.5	17.8	8.0	7.7
Eighth	17.7	18.5	7.9	7.8
Ninth	17.6	18.4	7.5	7.7
Tenth	19.2	16.4	6.6	6.9
All deciles[c]	17.9	17.7	8.0	7.6

Source: Brookings MERGE files.
a. Variant 1c is the most progressive and 3b is the least progressive set of incidence assumptions used in this study.
b. Includes only units in the sixth to tenth percentiles.
c. Includes negative incomes not shown separately.

and local taxes declined slightly as a share of income during this period, but the decline was distributed throughout the income scale and thus did not alter the U-shaped character of the effective rate curve under this variant (table 5-4).

Federal taxes are much less progressive under variant 3b than under 1c, while state and local taxes are distinctly regressive under 3b. Between 1966 and 1985, federal taxes became even less progressive under variant 3b, while state and local taxes became somewhat less regressive.

Taxes on Sources and Uses of Income

The data in the MERGE files permit an allocation of the burden of taxation among the sources and uses of income, as shown in table 5-5.[6] In 1966, the tax burden under variant 1c was almost twice as heavy on capital income than it was on labor income—33.0 percent versus 17.6 percent. The burden on capital income declined by almost 50 percent from 1966 to 1985, while the burden on labor income rose slightly. Thus labor income was taxed more heavily than capital income in 1985—20.6 percent versus 17.5 percent (table 5-5).

The shift in tax burdens from capital to labor income between 1966 and 1985 is even more dramatic under variant 3b, which distributes a major share of the corporation income, property, and payroll taxes to consumption. Under this variant, the effective rate of tax was slightly larger on capital income than on labor income in 1966, but in 1985 it was almost twice as large on labor income.

As might be expected, the effective tax rate on consumption is much lower than it is on either capital or labor income under variant 1c. By contrast, under variant 3b, consumption is taxed about as heavily as labor income in all years, almost as heavily as capital income in 1966 and 1970, and much more heavily thereafter. Under both variants, the tax on consumption rose from 1966 to 1975 and then declined from 1975 to 1985, ending the period at a somewhat lower level than at the beginning.

Changes in the Distribution of Income

The effect of changes in relative tax burdens on the distribution of income since 1966 is shown in table 5-6. To highlight changes in broad segments of the distribution, the income shares shown in this table are by quintiles rather than by deciles of the population.

According to the data in table 5-6, the distribution of income *before* taxes remained virtually unchanged from 1966 to 1985. There were small variations in the income shares received by the various quintiles, but these variations

6. In these calculations taxes were allocated to labor income, income from capital, or consumption in proportion to the amounts assumed to be subject to tax. Farm income and nonfarm business income were assumed to represent partly a return to labor and partly a return to capital. All taxes were allocated in accordance with the particular assumptions applicable to each incidence variant. For details see Joseph A. Pechman and Benjamin A. Okner, *Who Bears the Tax Burden?* (Brookings, 1974), pp. 79–80.

Table 5-5. *Effective Rates of Federal, State, and Local Taxes on Sources and Uses of Income under Variants 1c and 3b, Selected Years, 1966-85*[a]

Percent

	Variant 1c			Variant 3b		
Year	Income from labor[b]	Income from capital[c]	Consumption[d]	Income from labor[b]	Income from capital[c]	Consumption[d]
1966	17.6	33.0	8.3	16.0	21.0	17.6
1970	19.7	29.4	9.8	18.0	19.7	19.1
1975	22.6	22.2	10.6	20.6	13.7	21.9
1980	19.9	21.5	9.7	18.1	14.4	20.5
1985	20.6	17.5	7.7	18.6	10.8	17.0

Sources: Brookings MERGE files. For an explanation of the methods used to allocate taxes among sources and uses of income see text note 6.

a. Variant 1c is the most progressive and 3b is the least progressive set of incidence assumptions used in this study.

b. The sum of wages, salaries, wage supplements, and portion of nonfarm and farm business income regarded as labor income.

c. The sum of interest, corporation profits before tax, rents, royalties, capital gains, and portion of nonfarm and farm business income regarded as capital income.

d. The sum of total expenditures on consumption items generally subject to state sales and excise taxes.

were unsystematic and tended to be reversed in later years. Thus, for example, the share of adjusted family income before taxes under variant 1c in the bottom quintile of the population rose from 3.9 percent in 1966 to 4.6 percent in 1975, and then declined to 4.2 percent in 1985. The before-tax share of the top quintile was 47.7 percent in 1966; it then declined to 46.5 percent in 1970, rose to 48.9 percent in 1980, and declined again to 47.7 percent in 1985.[7]

It should be noted that adjusted family income includes transfer payments, which increased sharply from 1966 to 1985. Consequently, the distribution of market incomes (that is, adjusted family incomes less transfers) must have become more unequal. Unfortunately, the change during this period cannot be provided because size distributions of market incomes were not tabulated from the 1966 and 1970 MERGE files.

Since the distribution of adjusted family income before tax remained unchanged and the tax system became less progressive, the distribution of income *after* taxes became somewhat more concentrated during this period. Under variant 1c, the after-tax income shares in the first two quintiles were virtually the same in 1966 and 1985, but the shares of the next two quintiles declined while the share of the top quintile rose.

7. The constancy of the before-tax distribution has been observed in data derived from field surveys, but these surveys understate the shares of top incomes in the income distribution. Since the highest incomes in the MERGE files were obtained from income tax returns that are a more accurate representation of the top tail of the distribution, the constancy of the income shares on the basis of these data is all the more remarkable.

Table 5-6. *Distribution of Adjusted Family Income before and after Federal,
State, and Local Taxes under Variants 1c and 3b, by Population Quintile,
Selected Years, 1966–85*[a]

Percent

Population quintile	1966	1970	1975	1980	1985
			Variant 1c		
Before tax					
First	3.9	4.1	4.6	4.1	4.2
Second	10.0	10.1	10.2	9.7	10.0
Third	16.3	16.2	15.6	15.4	15.8
Fourth	22.0	23.0	21.8	21.9	23.3
Fifth	47.7	46.5	47.9	48.9	47.7
After tax					
First	4.3	n.a.	4.8	4.3	4.4
Second	10.3	n.a.	10.5	10.1	10.2
Third	16.4	n.a.	15.8	15.6	15.8
Fourth	23.3	n.a.	22.0	22.0	22.4
Fifth	45.7	n.a.	46.8	48.0	47.3
			Variant 3b		
Before tax					
First	4.0	4.1	4.6	4.1	4.2
Second	10.2	10.2	10.3	9.8	10.0
Third	16.7	16.5	15.8	15.6	15.9
Fourth	22.6	23.5	22.1	22.1	22.5
Fifth	46.6	45.7	47.2	48.4	47.3
After tax					
First	4.1	n.a.	4.6	4.1	4.2
Second	10.1	n.a.	10.4	9.9	10.0
Third	16.3	n.a.	15.7	15.4	15.6
Fourth	23.2	n.a.	21.9	21.8	22.2
Fifth	46.3	n.a.	47.5	48.8	48.0

Source: Brookings MERGE files. Figures are rounded.
n.a. Not available.
a. Variant 1c is the most progressive and 3b is the least progressive set of incidence assumptions used in this study. The
cumulative percentages are based on distributions of adjusted family income before tax and then reranked by adjusted family
income after tax.

Similar conclusions may be drawn from the distributions calculated under
the variant 3b assumptions. The income shares before tax of the bottom
quintile were 4.0 percent in 1966 and 4.2 percent in 1985; the shares of the
top quintile in these years were 46.6 percent and 47.3 percent, respectively.
While the after-tax shares of the bottom quintiles remained virtually unchanged between 1966 and 1985 and the shares of the next two quintiles
declined, that of the top quintile rose from 46.3 percent in 1966 to 48.0
percent in 1985.

Summary

The distribution of total tax burdens was less progressive in 1985 than in 1966 under the most progressive incidence assumptions and more regressive under the least progressive assumptions. This was the result mainly of the rise in payroll tax rates, which increased tax burdens at the lower end of the income scale, and the reduction in corporation income and property taxes, which reduced tax burdens at the top end. The individual and corporation income tax cuts enacted in 1981 also contributed to the decline in progressivity.

Federal taxes declined in progressivity between 1966 and 1985, while the burden of state and local taxes remained either U-shaped or regressive, depending on the incidence assumptions.

Taxes on capital income were heavier than those on labor income in 1966, but as a result of the reductions in the corporation income and property taxes, the tax burden on labor income was higher in 1985. Taxes on consumption were twice as high or higher under the least progressive incidence assumptions than under the most progressive.

The distribution of income *before* taxes was virtually the same in 1985 as it was in 1966. As a result of the decline in the progressivity of the tax system, the distribution of income *after* taxes was more unequal in 1985.

Statistical Tables

THE EFFECTIVE RATES of the major tax sources, by population decile, are given in this appendix for variants 1c and 3b in 1966, 1970, 1975, and 1985. Comparable data for 1980 appear in table 4-10.

Effective rates based on the other incidence variants shown in table 3-1 and more detailed breakdowns of the tax and income data are available from the author on request.

FEDERAL TAX POLICY
(Fourth Edition)
JOSEPH A. PECHMAN

This is a concise, nontechnical book for general readers and students interested in taxation as an instrument of public policy. Thoroughly revised and updated, this edition of a widely acclaimed classic reflects the major changes in the tax laws since 1976 and emphasizes current issues: tax limitations by state governments, inflation adjustments in income taxation, comprehensive income taxation, graduated income taxes versus expenditure taxes, the effects of taxation on economic incentives, and changes in the fiscal relations between the federal and state and local governments.

The author presents and evaluates contrasting views on most forms of taxation: personal and corporation income, general and selective consumption, payroll, estate and gift, property, and state and local. He also provides a useful analysis of the process of tax legislation and the role of taxation in fiscal policy. This book is the eighteenth publication in the second series of Brookings Studies of Government Finance.

Comments on the previous editions:
". . . a gem as an introduction to the subject—a shining combination of good writing and good thinking." *National Tax Journal*

"Pechman demonstrates again his ability to clarify both the fiscal and social significance of U.S. tax policy. This third edition . . . is crammed with useful information for officials, economists, and taxpayers." *The Wilson Quarterly*

". . . retains the same eminently readable style. The author again manages to summarize policy issues in clear and concise manner and without repressing his own viewpoint. Written to inform the nonexpert, the book provides valuable insights for expert and nonexpert alike." *Journal of Finance*

410 pp/1983/cloth and paper

Table A-1. *Effective Rates of Specific Federal, State, and Local Taxes,
Variants 1c and 3b, by Population Decile, 1966*[a]

Percent

Population decile	Individual income taxes	Corporation income tax	Property tax	Sales and excise taxes	Payroll taxes	Personal property and motor vehicle taxes	Total taxes
			Variant 1c				
First[b]	1.1	1.7	2.1	8.9	2.6	0.4	16.8
Second	2.3	2.1	2.6	7.8	3.8	0.4	18.9
Third	4.0	2.2	2.6	7.1	5.4	0.4	21.7
Fourth	5.4	1.9	2.1	6.7	6.1	0.4	22.6
Fifth	6.3	1.7	1.8	6.4	6.3	0.3	22.8
Sixth	7.0	1.5	1.6	6.1	6.2	0.3	22.7
Seventh	7.5	1.6	1.7	5.7	5.8	0.3	22.7
Eighth	8.3	1.8	1.8	5.5	5.4	0.3	23.1
Ninth	8.8	2.2	2.2	5.0	4.8	0.3	23.3
Tenth	11.4	8.1	5.1	3.2	2.2	0.2	30.1
Top 5 percent	12.3	10.2	6.1	2.6	1.4	0.1	32.7
Top 1 percent	14.4	15.2	7.8	1.7	0.4	0.1	39.6
All deciles[c]	8.5	3.9	3.0	5.1	4.4	0.3	25.2
			Variant 3b				
First[b]	1.2	6.1	6.4	8.9	4.5	0.4	27.5
Second	2.0	5.4	5.1	7.5	4.5	0.4	24.8
Third	3.9	5.0	4.6	6.8	5.4	0.4	26.0
Fourth	5.1	4.4	3.8	6.5	5.7	0.3	25.9
Fifth	6.0	4.1	3.3	6.2	5.8	0.3	25.8
Sixth	6.7	3.9	3.2	5.9	5.6	0.3	25.6
Seventh	7.3	3.7	3.2	5.6	5.4	0.3	25.5
Eighth	8.0	3.7	3.2	5.3	5.0	0.3	25.5
Ninth	8.4	3.9	3.2	4.9	4.5	0.3	25.1
Tenth	11.9	5.2	2.9	3.3	2.5	0.2	25.9
Top 5 percent	13.1	5.7	2.9	2.8	1.9	0.1	26.6
Top 1 percent	16.4	6.9	2.5	2.0	0.9	0.1	28.9
All deciles[c]	8.4	4.4	3.4	5.0	4.4	0.3	25.9

Source: Brookings 1966 MERGE file. For an explanation of the incidence variants see table 3-1.
a. Variant 1c is the most progressive and 3b the least progressive set of incidence assumptions examined in this study.
b. Includes only units in the sixth to tenth percentiles.
c. Includes negative incomes not shown separately.

Table A-2. *Effective Rates of Specific Federal, State, and Local Taxes,*
Variants 1c and 3b, by Population Decile, 1970[a]

Percent

Population decile	Individual income taxes	Corporation income tax	Property tax	Sales and excise taxes	Payroll taxes	Personal property and motor vehicle taxes	Total taxes
				Variant 1c			
First[b]	3.1	1.9	3.6	7.6	2.2	0.5	18.8
Second	3.5	1.8	3.4	7.1	3.2	0.4	19.5
Third	4.0	1.5	2.8	7.2	4.8	0.4	20.8
Fourth	5.8	1.4	2.5	6.9	6.3	0.4	23.2
Fifth	6.8	1.3	2.2	6.7	6.8	0.3	24.0
Sixth	7.6	1.1	2.1	6.3	6.7	0.3	24.1
Seventh	8.2	1.2	2.1	6.0	6.4	0.3	24.3
Eighth	9.1	1.4	2.2	5.6	5.9	0.3	24.6
Ninth	10.3	1.6	2.3	5.1	5.4	0.3	25.0
Tenth	13.8	5.3	5.3	3.5	2.7	0.2	30.7
Top 5 percent	15.0	6.8	6.4	2.9	1.8	0.2	33.0
Top 1 percent	17.0	10.6	8.9	1.9	0.4	0.1	39.0
All deciles[c]	9.7	2.6	3.3	5.3	4.9	0.3	26.1
				Variant 3b			
First[b]	3.1	4.0	7.3	7.5	3.5	0.5	25.9
Second	3.4	3.5	5.9	7.0	3.9	0.4	24.2
Third	3.8	3.2	4.8	7.0	5.0	0.4	24.1
Fourth	5.6	3.0	4.2	6.8	6.0	0.3	25.8
Fifth	6.6	2.7	3.8	6.5	6.4	0.3	26.4
Sixth	7.3	2.7	3.7	6.1	6.1	0.3	26.3
Seventh	8.0	2.7	3.6	5.8	5.9	0.3	26.2
Eighth	9.0	2.6	3.4	5.5	5.5	0.3	26.4
Ninth	10.0	2.5	3.1	5.0	5.2	0.3	26.1
Tenth	14.2	3.4	3.4	3.6	3.0	0.2	27.8
Top 5 percent	15.6	3.8	3.5	3.1	2.3	0.2	28.5
Top 1 percent	19.0	4.8	3.8	2.1	1.1	0.1	30.9
All deciles[c]	9.7	3.0	3.7	5.3	4.8	0.3	26.7

Source: Brookings 1970 MERGE file. For an explanation of the incidence variants see table 3-1.

a. Variant 1c is the most progressive and 3b the least progressive set of incidence assumptions examined in this study.

b. Includes only units in the sixth to tenth percentiles.

c. Includes negative incomes not shown separately.

Table A-3. *Effective Rates of Specific Federal, State, and Local Taxes,*
Variants 1c and 3b, by Population Decile, 1975[a]

Percent

Population decile	Individual income taxes	Corporation income tax	Property tax	Sales and excise taxes	Payroll taxes	Personal property and motor vehicle taxes	Total taxes
			Variant 1c				
First[b]	2.8	0.6	0.9	9.2	7.6	0.2	21.2
Second	3.9	0.6	0.9	7.1	7.3	0.1	19.9
Third	5.1	0.8	1.2	6.1	7.0	0.2	20.5
Fourth	6.5	0.8	1.3	6.0	7.1	0.2	22.0
Fifth	7.3	1.0	1.5	5.7	7.1	0.3	23.0
Sixth	7.8	1.1	1.7	5.5	6.9	0.3	23.3
Seventh	8.3	1.1	1.8	5.2	6.8	0.3	23.6
Eighth	9.2	1.3	2.0	5.0	6.6	0.3	24.4
Ninth	10.3	1.6	2.3	4.5	6.2	0.3	25.3
Tenth	11.7	4.9	4.6	2.4	3.3	0.2	27.1
Top 5 percent	12.0	6.0	5.2	1.9	2.3	0.1	27.6
Top 1 percent	12.3	7.8	6.2	1.1	1.0	0.1	28.5
All deciles[c]	9.3	2.5	2.8	4.5	5.7	0.3	25.0
			Variant 3b				
First[b]	2.6	4.0	4.7	9.6	8.5	0.2	29.6
Second	3.7	2.8	3.4	6.8	7.3	0.1	24.2
Third	4.8	2.5	2.7	5.6	6.5	0.2	22.2
Fourth	6.2	2.6	2.8	5.9	6.8	0.2	24.6
Fifth	7.1	2.6	2.9	5.6	6.7	0.3	25.3
Sixth	7.6	2.6	3.0	5.3	6.5	0.3	25.3
Seventh	8.1	2.6	3.1	5.1	6.4	0.3	25.5
Eighth	9.0	2.5	3.1	4.8	6.2	0.3	26.0
Ninth	10.1	2.6	3.3	4.3	5.7	0.3	26.3
Tenth	12.0	3.1	3.2	2.5	3.2	0.2	24.2
Top 5 percent	12.5	3.2	3.1	2.0	2.4	0.2	23.4
Top 1 percent	13.0	3.5	2.9	1.2	1.2	0.1	21.9
All deciles[c]	9.3	2.8	3.2	4.5	5.5	0.3	25.5

Source: Brookings 1975 MERGE file. For an explanation of the incidence variants see table 3-1.

a. Variant 1c is the most progressive and 3b the least progressive set of incidence assumptions examined in this study.

b. Includes only units in the sixth to tenth percentiles.

c. Includes negative incomes not shown separately.

Table A-4. *Effective Rates of Specific Federal, State, and Local Taxes, Variants 1c and 3b, by Population Decile, 1985*[a]

Percent

Population decile	Individual income taxes	Corporation income tax	Property tax	Sales and excise taxes	Payroll taxes	Personal property and motor vehicle taxes	Total taxes
			Variant 1c				
First[b]	4.2	0.5	0.7	7.0	9.4	0.1	21.9
Second	5.5	0.5	0.7	5.9	8.7	0.1	21.3
Third	6.9	0.6	0.9	5.0	7.9	0.1	21.4
Fourth	8.2	0.6	0.9	4.6	7.9	0.2	22.5
Fifth	9.1	0.7	1.0	4.3	7.8	0.2	23.1
Sixth	9.8	0.8	1.2	4.1	7.5	0.2	23.5
Seventh	10.3	0.8	1.3	3.9	7.2	0.2	23.7
Eighth	11.4	0.9	1.3	3.7	7.0	0.2	24.6
Ninth	12.2	1.2	1.7	3.3	6.4	0.2	25.1
Tenth	12.7	3.6	3.3	1.9	3.6	0.1	25.3
Top 5 percent	12.7	4.5	3.8	1.5	2.6	0.1	25.2
Top 1 percent	12.8	5.7	4.4	1.1	1.4	0.1	25.5
All deciles[c]	10.9	1.8	2.0	3.4	6.2	0.2	24.5
			Variant 3b				
First[b]	4.1	2.8	3.3	7.2	10.8	0.1	28.2
Second	5.4	2.3	2.5	5.7	9.5	0.1	25.6
Third	6.8	2.0	2.1	4.9	8.6	0.1	24.6
Fourth	8.1	1.9	2.1	4.6	8.4	0.2	25.2
Fifth	8.9	1.9	2.1	4.2	8.1	0.2	25.3
Sixth	9.6	1.9	2.1	4.0	7.8	0.2	25.6
Seventh	10.0	1.9	2.1	3.8	7.4	0.2	25.4
Eighth	11.2	1.8	2.2	3.7	7.2	0.2	26.3
Ninth	12.0	1.9	2.3	3.2	6.5	0.2	26.1
Tenth	12.9	2.3	2.3	1.9	3.8	0.1	23.3
Top 5 percent	13.1	2.4	2.3	1.6	2.9	0.1	22.4
Top 1 percent	13.4	2.6	2.2	1.1	1.8	0.1	21.2
All deciles[c]	10.9	2.1	2.3	3.4	6.5	0.2	25.3

Source: Brookings 1985 MERGE file. For an explanation of the incidence variants see table 3-1.
a. Variant 1c is the most progressive and 3b the least progressive set of incidence assumptions examined in this study.
b. Includes only units in the sixth to tenth percentiles.
c. Includes negative incomes not shown separately.

Index

Aaron, Henry, 3, 25n, 30n, 50n
Accelerated cost recovery system
(ACRS), 65
Accelerated depreciation range (ADR),
64, 65
Accounting period, tax burdens and, 48–
51
ACRS. *See* Accelerated cost recovery
system.
ADR. *See* Accelerated depreciation
range.
Allocation of taxes. *See* Taxes, allocation
of
Annuities, 13
Assets: capital gains and, 13, 22; income
and capital, 12; rate of return on, 34

Bailey, Martin J., 13n, 28n
Bequests and gifts, 12
Bishop, George A., 19n
Bonds, 22
Boskin, Michael J., 28n, 29n, 30n, 36n
Bosworth, Barry P., 28n
Bracket creep, 8
Brittain, John A., 25n, 27n, 31n
Brown, Harry Gunnison, 23n
Browning, Edgar K., 29n, 35n, 50n
Business taxes. *See* Indirect business
taxes

Capital, 31; corporation income tax as
tax on, 7, 26n, 29, 31–32, 38–39, 40,
72, 75; property tax as tax on, 7; study
assumptions and, 36; tax burden analysis and income on, 6, 8, 37, 72; tax
incidence theory and, 25
Capital gains, 12–13
Carliner, Geoffrey, 30n
Case, Karl E., 27n
Colm, Gerhard, 23n
Competition, 25
Consumers, 23, 24, 36, 39; data on, 20–
21, 22; effective tax rates and, 10;
property tax on improvements and, 6;

sales and excise taxes and, 6n; tax
incidence and, 25–26
Consumption: data on, 22; effective tax
rate on, 72; family expenditures on,
24, 50; money, 40–41; taxes and, 25–
26
Consumption patterns, 3, 26
Consumption tax, 7, 24, 28n, 33, 36,
38–39, 40, 70, 72
Corporate stock. *See* Stock, corporate.
See also Stockholders
Corporation income tax, 10, 23, 36, 41,
61, 67, 75; changes in tax burden and,
8, 9; income and taxes and, 38–39;
legislative history and, 63–64; stockholders and, 40; tax burden in *1980*
and, 6–7, 8, 46, 47, 57; tax cuts and,
70; tax incidence theory and, 29, 30,
31–32. *See also* Individual income tax
Cragg, John G., 33n
Customs duties, 14, 16

Data: study, 1–2; tax and consumer, 20–
21
David, Paul A., 28n
Davies, James, 51n
Death taxes. *See* Estate and gift taxes
Deaton, Angus, 49n
de Leeuw, Frank, 30n
Demographics, 7n
Denison, Edward F., 28n
Distribution of income. *See* Income dis-
tribution
Dividends, 13, 57n

Earnings. *See* Labor income
Effective tax rates, 45–46, 46n, 47, 56–
57, 59–61, 64, 67–72; changes in tax
burden and progressivity and, 8; consumption and, 72; defining, 18–19;
federal and state taxes and, 59–60, 70–
71; income and, 6; individual income
tax and, 55; progressivity or regressivity and, 46, 57; ranking in *1980,* 3; the

81

rich and, 10; statistical tables on, 76–
80; tax burden and, 47
Employees, 23, 37, 55; payroll taxes
and, 6n, 31, 36, 38
Employers, 31, 36, 38, 55
Employment (full), 25, 26n, 28
Equilibrium models, 25
Equity, 1
Estate and gift taxes, 14, 16; income
and, 2n

Families: allocation of taxes and, 39–41;
corporate stock and, 16; defined, 2n;
defining income of, 13–14; income
and, 1, 18, 21, 37–38; income and tax
burden and, 49–51; income distribution and, 42
Farm assets, 13, 22. See also Assets
Federal taxes: cuts in, 69–70; defining
taxes and, 14–15, 17; government
expenditures and, 26–27; individual
income tax and, 6; legislative history
and, 63–67; progressivity and, 8, 71,
75; state and local taxes and, 59–60
Feldstein, Martin, 29n, 30n, 36n, 50n

Galper, Harvey, 39n
Gifts and bequests, 12
Gift taxes. See Estate and gift taxes
Gillespie, W. Irwin, 23n
Goode, Richard, 32n
Government. See Federal taxes; State
and local taxes
Guitton, H., 3n

Harberger, Arnold C., 23n, 24n, 28n,
33n
Hausman, Jerry, 25n, 28n, 36n
Herriot, Roger A., 23n
High-income persons and groups, 43–44
Housing, 30; property tax on improve-
ments and, 6
Housing expenditures, 50
Howrey, E. Philip, 28n
Hymans, Saul H., 28n

Incidence. See Tax incidence
Incidence assumptions. See Tax incidence assumptions
Income: allocation of taxes and, 39–41;
on capital, 8; by class, 39–41; concept
of money, 20; consumer data matched
with tax data and, 20–22; defining,
11–14; effective tax rates and, 18;
family, 1, 2n, 13–14, 16, 18, 21, 37–
38, 39, 42–43; family economic deci-

sions and, 49–51; income distribution
and tax burden and, 42–44, 73, 74;
income tax and, 66; MERGE file and,
2–3; money, 42, 44; property, 6, 8,
36, 37, 40, 46; tax burden analysis
and, 5; taxes and, 37–39; taxes on
sources of, 72; tax incidence and, 24,
26. See also specific income categories
Income distribution, 3; changes in tax
burden and, 9–10, 72–74; effect of
taxes and transfers on, 51–52; effect
on taxes on, 1; measurement procedures and, 19; tax burden and, 42–44,
60–62; tax burden distribution and,
44–51; tax system and, 4–5, 10
Income tax. See Corporation income tax;
Individual income tax
Indirect business taxes, 17, 39, 40, 42
Individual income tax, 23, 66, 69, 75;
allocation and, 41; defining taxes and,
17; government reliance on, 6; income
and taxes and, 38; MERGE and, 39–
40; progressivity and, 8; study
assumptions and, 34; tax burden analysis and, 53–55; tax incidence theory
and, 27–28. See also Corporate
income tax
Individual retirement accounts (IRAs),
64, 65, 70
Insurance, interest on, 22
Insurance system, private, 14n
Interest, 22, 57n
Inventories, 13
Inventory valuation, 14n
Investment, 33
IRA. See Individual retirement accounts

Johnson, William R., 29n, 35n, 50n

Keoghs, 65, 70
Krzyzaniak, Marian, 32n, 33n

Labor income, 75; payroll taxes and, 31;
study assumptions and, 35–36; tax
burden analysis and, 8, 37, 72; tax incidence theory and, 25, 34
Landowners, 29–30
Land, property tax on, 6n, 23, 29–30,
33–34. See also Property tax
Leonard, Herman, 27n
Local government. See State and local
taxes

McGuire, Martin, 3n
McLure, Charles E., Jr., 24n
Margolis, J., 3n

DATE DUE			